WHY WE
SELF-SABOTAGE

Why We Self-Sabotage

DEBORAH D. DELBRIDGE

CovenantBridge Publishing

First Printing, 2023 - CovenantBridge Publishing

ISBN 979-8-9862183-6-6

Copy-editing:
Allison Elliot, Bree Moffett, and Debra Moffett

Contents

Chapter 1

The Saboteur Within

We all have goals we would love to achieve. Many of us have hopes and aspirations of a better career, a bigger bank account, harmonious relationships, good health, and a significant and notable life. We want to make a difference in the world. We want our life to mean something. We want to be used by God to help the planet.

When we consider why we don't accomplish some of our goals, human nature wants to blame our circumstances, other people, bad luck, the devil, or the timing of God. Our immediate reaction is to point our finger at all these peripheral roadblocks instead of recognizing that we are often the ones that stop our forward momentum. We are the ones who self-sabotage our success way more than any external factor.

This chapter will discuss some surface level reasons we self-sabotage. The rest of the book will discuss some deeper subconscious root causes of self-sabotage.

Fear

When fear stops us from taking steps towards our goals, we usually don't recognize and label it as fear. Instead, we have excuses that point to other issues.

Some objectives require additional training, a certification, or a degree. We may blame our delay on a lack of funds for the schooling, or we may attribute the stall to our busy schedule. Those reasons help us feel better about our lack of advancement, but the truth is, we could do it if we pushed ourselves.

Between 1997 and 1999, I worked full time, I attended a Bible School, and I took all the courses necessary to get my Broker's license in real estate. Was that a lot on my plate at one time? Yes, but when we follow the leading of the Holy Spirit, He gives us grace to do it.

Convincing ourselves we are too busy can be a way to mask fear. Or persuading ourselves that money is too tight to add tuition can be another way to mask fear. There will always be reasons why it isn't the right time to go back to school. But, often those excuses cover up fear of change.

Fear is a liar. Recognize that the enemy of our soul, the devil and his minions, use fear as their primary tool to keep us complacent, immobile, and defeated. Yes, going back to school, or starting a business, or asking a woman out on a date, can all be very intimidating. But there won't be advancement unless there is risk. Risk is scary but there will be no reward without it.

Procrastination

Some people live their entire life procrastinating. Then they wake up at 50 years old and discover that they have wasted their life.

My brother Ken was a lifelong procrastinator. After graduating from high school, he took one college class. Every year from 18 years old to 27 years old, he would register for college classes (because that was a requirement to live under my father's roof) but would end up dropping out of the classes. He always gave the excuse that he would do it the following semester or year.

He was a good handyman and electrician, but he

never got his certification as an electrician, so he was forced to take small handyman jobs instead of larger electrical contracts. He signed up for the courses a few times, but never completed the courses. Before he passed away in 2021, I had several conversations with him, and he lamented that he wasted his life.

He had big dreams. He wrote some amazing song lyrics, and his lifelong goal was for at least one of his songs to make it big. But he never took any action to make that happen. He was never married because he procrastinated having a social life. He really sabotaged every area of his life with procrastination.

Miracles usually don't just fall in our lap. We have to take small and large actions towards our goals. Procrastination is a lie. There are a lot of things we can't do tomorrow. Some activities and steps need to be taken now or we will miss opportunities for advancement.

Weariness

Sometimes our tank is empty. I get it. Sometimes we are physically and emotionally exhausted. If we had to admit it, we would even say we are discouraged. We may not be in the right frame of mind to conquer. When we lift our foot to take a step forward, we find that we took a step back instead.

Life can seem like we are on a hamster wheel at times. We are exerting all our time and energy and we aren't going anywhere. We are just spinning in circles and it's tiring.

If we feel tired all the time, maybe we should re-evaluate our schedule. Are there unnecessary activities that are wasting our time. Are there relationships that are emotionally draining us? Is it possible to schedule some down time?

If you are feeling exhausted, I encourage you to go to church. The logical option would be to skip it and sleep in. Being in a church service, that has anointed praise and worship, can rejuvenate your soul, and charge your emotional and spiritual batteries.

It's okay to take some self-care time when you're weary. But that season of exhaustion shouldn't be a long period of time. That weariness can turn into a habit where your soul gets used to it, so it responds in tiredness all the time. And the demon assigned to you can try to trick your emotions into believing you are tired all the time to keep you dormant. Get rest but then get up and move forward.

Our Flesh Nature

Let's face it, our flesh has a voice. We would much rather sleep in for an extra half hour than get up and hop on the treadmill. We would rather eat that extra few bites of pasta than watch our portions. We would rather binge watch Netflix than do the dishes or laundry.

Our carnal, Adamic nature partners with procrastination and we give ourselves excuses to *eat, drink and be merry* while we, oftentimes, neglect necessary duties. That neglect isn't just with household or personal health goals, it can affect our work and ministries goals.

It is good for us spiritually to put our flesh under subjection. It is good to fast or make ourselves exercise. It tells our flesh that it isn't the boss. It makes us feel empowered when we deny our flesh and make strides towards our goals.

Self-Sabotage

We self-sabotage when we do or think something that prevents us from achieving what we want or what is good for us. Everyone contends with self-sabotage. A person may be successful in the business world, but they are weak in their relationships with their family. Another person may be diligent with diet and exercise, but they sabotage opportunities for financial success. A person can be a spiritual leader and still self-sabotage their goals.

The apostle Paul, who wrote two thirds of the New Testament, struggled with self-sabotage. He wrote about it in Romans 7. Romans 7:15 says, *"For what I am doing, I do not understand. For what I will to do, that I do not practice; but what I hate, that I do."*

We are all a work in progress. I don't know anyone that feels like they are excelling in every area of their life.

Will you become a perfect person after reading this book? Of course not. But I believe this book will bring a new level of understanding. I believe it can help supply some of those missing pieces of the puzzle so that you can obtain new levels of success. Fear, procrastination, weariness, and our flesh nature are all things that we assume cause us to self-sabotage. But the real root causes are subconscious which this book will explore in a deeper level.

Chapter 2

Understanding Our Soul

Most Christians would embrace the concept that mankind is a three-part being. We are a spirit. We have a soul. And we live in a body. That definition has been around for decades. Our soul contains our mind, will, emotions, intellect, memory, and creativity. Our spirit becomes the house where the Holy Spirit resides when we accept Jesus Christ as our savior and make Him Lord of our lives.

The phrase *subconscious mind* isn't in the Bible. It is a psychological term, and it isn't discussed very much in Christian teaching. Christian scholars and pastors don't deny that the subconscious mind exists, they just haven't known how to define it since that term is not in the Bible. The Bible does teach us about the subconscious mind which will be discussed in this chapter. But, for the most part, the Bible uses terms like *heart, mind, soul,* and *spirit* to describe the different parts of our human psyche. Oftentimes, when the Bible uses the term *heart*, it is talking about our subconscious mind. Other times, it seems the terms *heart, soul, mind,* and *spirit* are almost used interchangeably, and it is up to the reader to determine the context of what is being taught.

When we accept Jesus in our heart, the Holy Spirit comes and resides in our human spirit. When we become born-again, we actually become a type of new species. We have the spirit of God living in us.

2 Corinthians 5:17 says, *"Therefore, if anyone is in Christ, he is a new creation; old things have passed away; behold all things have become new."* We become a new spiritual force on the Earth. As children of God, we carry spiritual authority as sons and daughters of the Most-High God.

However, very few Christians throughout history have tapped into the spiritual authority that God has endued us with. It wasn't their fault. They operated in the knowledge they had. Spiritual knowledge and understanding has increased significantly since the dark ages. Our generation has the capacity to walk as sons and daughter of God in a much greater dimension than believers before us because we have so much more teaching and revelational knowledge available to us.

We need to get a fresh revelation that God dwells within us. We are not mere men. We are a royal priesthood that was chosen for *such a time as this* to be in God's end-time army. Each of us has been hand-picked and equipped to carry out specific duties and assignments for God.

When God Speaks

If God dwells in us and is all-knowing, why aren't we all-knowing? If God speaks to us, why can't we hear His voice? There are three main reasons for it:

1) We are not meant to be all-knowing. God requires faith and if we knew the answers to all of our questions, then we wouldn't use faith in our journey here on Earth. As well, if we were all-knowing, we would probably try to interfere in situations that are none of our business.

2) Most people haven't developed their spiritual discernment. Most believers don't pay attention to the random thoughts that cross their minds. They don't know how to recognize the Holy Spirit's voice, the voice of demonic suggestion, or their own human voice of reasoning and rationalizing.

3) When God speaks to us, it usually isn't with an audible voice or through a burning bush like with Moses. Now that we have the Holy Spirit in us, the Holy Spirit speaks from our spirit. We may not hear what God is trying to tell us because there is a chasm between our human spirit where the Holy Spirit resides and our conscious mind. The message from the Holy Spirit has to travel from our human spirit and through our subconscious mind, before we register it as a thought in our conscious mind. If we have a lot of junk in our subconscious mind, that message from the Holy Spirit can get blocked or distorted.

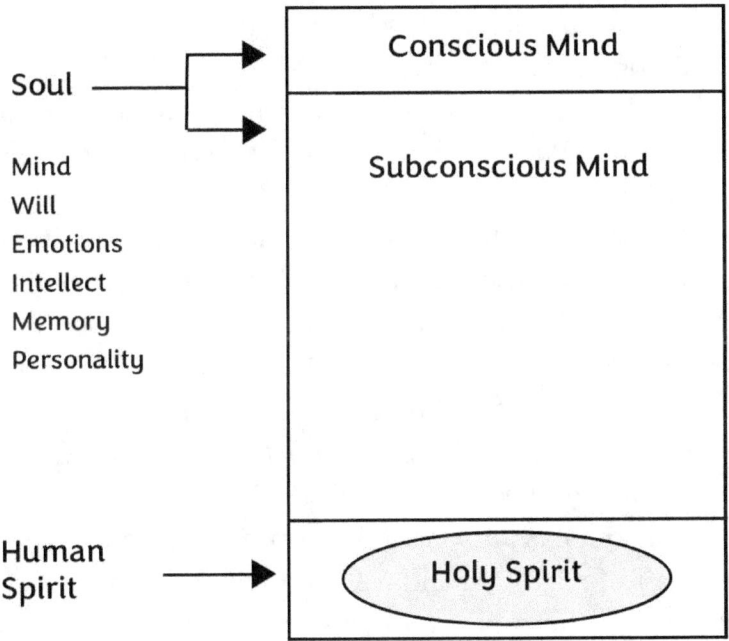

Soul

Mind
Will
Emotions
Intellect
Memory
Personality

Human Spirit

Conscious Mind

Subconscious Mind

Holy Spirit

It can be confusing for new Christians. They hear verses like 2 Corinthians 5:17 where it says we have been made brand new, and they think there may be something wrong with them. While some addictions or bad habits may have fallen away when they accepted Jesus in their heart, they still have some negative thoughts and behaviors. For some people, it may seem like a contradiction. Are they clean and righteous or do they need to battle their sin nature?

If we understand the different components of our human psyche, it can help us understand it a little better. At the bottom of the graphic, we see the Holy Spirit dwelling in our human spirit. The core of who we are is changed and made anew. We now have divinity living in us.

So, if we are a new creation, why do we still have a sin nature? We have been made righteous, so why do we still think and act ungodly?

Our soul still has a carnal, Adamic nature that we need to *"renew to the word of God"* (in Christian terms, Romans 12:2) or clean up and educate (in worldly terms). Romans 12:2 says, *"And do not be conformed to this world but be transformed by the renewing of your mind, that you may prove what is that good and acceptable and perfect will of God."*

Our soul has two parts, our conscious mind and our subconscious mind, and we need to renew both areas. Renewing our mind isn't just memorizing a handful of Bible verses. Yes, we need to get God's word in us, but we also need to root out our sinful and self-sabotaging thoughts and behaviors.

When our minds are renewed to the word of God, we are able to *walk in the spirit*. That doesn't mean we will be perfect, but it means our discernment will be tuned into the voice of the Holy Spirit. We will obey the direct commands and the subtle inklings we think He is telling us. God, oftentimes, uses scripture to speak to us. If we know Bible stories and scriptures, the Holy Spirit will bring that story or scripture to our remembrance when He is trying to give us understanding of an issue or direction with a problem.

Our Subconscious Mind

Psychology tells us that 10% of our mind is our conscious mind and the other 90% is our subconscious mind. I assume they use those percentages because we, allegedly, only use 10% of our brain. The percentages aren't relevant, but everyone would agree that we have a conscious mind and a subconscious mind. Psychology also tells us that our beliefs, behaviors, and true motives are driven from our subconscious mind. And the Bible agrees with that, which I'm going to demonstrate in this section.

While the Bible doesn't use the term *subconscious mind*, there is a verse in the Bible that defines the two sections of our soul. Hebrews 4:12 reads, *"For the word of God is living and powerful, and sharper than a two-edged sword, piercing even the division between soul and spirit, and of joints and marrow, and is a discerner of the thoughts and intents of the heart."*

Before I dissect and download information out of this verse, I want to first comment on the first part of this scripture. It says the word of God is *"living and powerful."* When we read the Bible, new revelations and insights can spring forth. The Holy Spirit can highlight a scripture that we have read a hundred times. He can breathe new life on it and cause us to see it in a slightly different way. When Martin Luther read *"the just shall live by faith"* in the Bible, suddenly a metaphorical lightbulb turned on. He had a fresh revelation that people are saved by faith and not works. In 1517, he accidently started the Protestant church when he posted his observations and objections to the door of the Catholic Church.

Even in the last hundred years, the church has gained insights and revelations that earlier Christians didn't have. Our spiritual understanding has increased with each new generation and revelational knowledge has come into the church. We now stand on the shoulders of the healing revival preachers that brought the church a new understanding of God's will to heal and restore. We stand on the shoulders of the *Word of Faith* teachers that taught us the importance of faith and standing on the Word.

The Holy Spirit can not only illuminate truths He wants the church to understand, He can also give personal correction, direction, and affection through the word. When we are synced up to the voice of the

Holy Spirit, He will direct our steps. He may prompt us to read a verse a second time to draw our attention to it. Then, we may read a post on social media that touches on the subject. In another instance, we may overhear a conversation in line at the grocery store, and we finally figure out that God is trying to get our attention about something. We then can go back and reread that verse God was trying to highlight to us and He gives us a new understanding of it, or He can give us guidance on how to handle a specific situation. The word of God is *living and powerful* and God uses the scriptures to lead and guide us every day.

Here's an example. In 1996, when I had just started working at Coldwell Banker Real Estate in Irvine, California, I attended a two-week sales training course. The first week, the instructor taught on accumulating lots of potential clients. She theorized that one out of seven potential buyers we work with, turns into a transaction. She had dozens of stuffed animal frogs and figurine frogs all around the room. Her theme was, "you have to kiss a lot of frogs before you find your prince." The frogs represented the potential clients and the more potential clients we worked with, the more transactions we would have.

On the Thursday morning of that first week, before I left for the training, the scripture reference of "Psalm 2" came to mind. It was very common, in that season, for the Holy Spirit to whisper a scripture address to me. Then, when I read the Bible verse or chapter, the Holy Spirit gave me correction, direction, or affection.

After I read the first part of Psalm 2:12 which reads, "Kiss the Son.", the Holy Spirit told me, "Kiss the Son and you won't have to kiss a lot of frogs."

I have always remembered that humorous encounter with God. It was God's way of reiterating Matthew 6:33 which tells us to seek first the kingdom of God and everything else will be added to us. I also got the sense that God was trying to tell me that I wouldn't have to waste my time with potential clients that were not ready, willing, or able to buy or sell a house. If my interaction with potential clients didn't end up in a transaction, then God had another purpose for the time I spent with them. Maybe I was there to offer them hope or guidance. It was a way that God communicated with me that I worked for Him and that I should be aware of that with every potential client that I interacted with.

Back in the mid-to-late 90's, when God was teaching me about *diseases of the soul*, the Holy Spirit spoke to me as I was reading Hebrews 12:4. As I was reading the verse one day, I sensed the Holy Spirit prompting me to examine the conjunctive phrases in the verse. Then, the Holy Spirit told me to put the conjunctive phrases into two columns. The conjunctions I am referring to are the "and" phrases in the second half of the verse. They read, *"piercing even the division between (soul and spirit), and of (joints and marrow), and is a discerner of the (thoughts and intents) of the heart."* When I did, a lightbulb flipped on in me. The Holy Spirit illuminated to me that the first column references our conscious mind, and the second column refers to our subconscious mind.

Conscious Mind		Subconscious Mind
Soul	and	Spirit
Joints	and	Marrow
Thoughts	and	Intents

Let's look at the first column. The conscious mind is where we think and reason. The Bible's metaphor of a body part describes it as *joint* because the conscious mind is where thoughts are joined together. It is where we reason, where we plan, where we create. The conscious mind is where we connect information, form opinions, organize conclusions, and judge situations. We *join* together our education with our creativity and think up new ideas, procedures, and strategies. That first column tells us that our conscious mind is where our *soul joins* our *thoughts* together.

The second column describes our subconscious mind. To reiterate, psychology tells us that our beliefs, behaviors, and true motives are driven from our subconscious mind. The word *intent* is another word for motive. So, it appears that the Bible and psychology are in agreement that true motives are originated in our subconscious mind. We may reason and rationalize our beliefs and behaviors in our conscious mind, but our true motives and intents are housed in our subconscious mind.

What is marrow? Marrow is the dark, pasty substance inside of bones. It is hidden and not visible. I think it is so interesting that the Holy Spirit inspired the writer of Hebrews to use these two body parts (joints and marrow) to describe something that he didn't fully understand at the time.

Marrow is that part of the body where red blood cells are produced. The blood that is produced in the marrow is the life force of the entire body. What is made in the hidden part of the body is what brings oxygen and life to every organ, limb, and capillary in the body. Likewise, that which is produced in the most hidden place of our soul, our subconscious mind, is what drives our beliefs and behaviors and can be witnessed in our words, thoughts, and actions.

The marrow also is where our immunity is strengthened. Our immunity fights sickness and disease, and it is what keeps us healthy. Naturally speaking, when there is disease in the bone marrow, it makes the body weak, sick, and frail. When our immunity is compromised and weak, it shows outwardly, and our poor health is evident for others to see. Likewise, when there is sickness and disease in our subconscious mind, our behavior becomes ugly and evident for others to see.

And lastly, the marrow is where blood platelets are produced. Blood platelets assist in blood clotting, so we don't bleed to death when we are injured. I find this fascinating because our subconscious mind also has types of emotional blood platelets. We have *emotional defense mechanisms* like denial, repression, compartmentalization, and others that shield us when we can't handle the full emotional impact of a situation. They stop our emotional bleeding until we can process the psychological trauma in our life.

The Rudder

A rudder is what steers a ship. If the rudder is off course, the ship will never reach its desired destination. James 3:4 says, *"Look at the ship: although they are so large and are driven by fierce winds, they are turned by a very small rudder whatever the pilot desires."* Just as a small rudder steers a huge ship, so our tongues steer our lives.

We frame our life by the words of our mouth. Matthew 15:18 says, *"But those things which proceed out of the mouth come from the heart, and they defile a man."* Luke 6:45 says: *"A good man out of the good treasure of his heart brings forth good; and an evil man out of the evil treasures of his heart brings forth evil. For out of the abundance of the heart his mouth speaks."*

What are good treasures and evil treasures of a person's heart? They are the good and bad blueprints that reside in a person's subconscious mind. If a person is jealous, prideful, and spiteful, it will come out in their speech. Their "evil" or negative character qualities will shape their relationships, their life choices, and their success level. Likewise, when a person is kind, generous, and loving, they will sow those good qualities into relationships and will reap the same. Our speech and actions are really the fruit of whatever trees we have growing in our subconscious mind. We may guard our speech around certain people but those who know us the best are the ones who witness what really is in us.

What is in Our Subconscious Mind?

Very few people have any knowledge of the subconscious mind. Most people don't know that the things in their subconscious mind really do shape their lives. Two people can go through the exact same trauma in their life. One person regresses and wallows in the trauma, while the other is able to succeed and thrive in life. Of course, a person's personality temperament has a bearing on how emotional trauma affects them. However, what a person has residing in their subconscious mind determines how they react and function. The decisions that are made, the beliefs that are embraced, and the actions that are taken are all rooted in what a person has in their subconscious mind.

Yes, we can attempt to make conscious decisions about our attitudes and actions after an offense or emotionally traumatic event. We may tell ourselves one thing in our mind, but ultimately, our attitudes and actions will track with what we believe in our heart. In other words, when we let our guard down, our actions will obey what has been branded and blueprinted in our subconscious mind.

Conscious Mind (10%)
. Reason and Rationalization
. Create and Strategize
Subconscious Mind (90%)
Our subconscious mind houses:
. Our Faith
. Our Rhema Promises and Impartations
. Our Aspirations, Hopes, and Dreams
. Our Personality Temperament
. Our Character Traits
. Our Comfort Zones and Subconscious Limitations
. Our Identity
. Our Fears and Insecurities
. Our Deep-rooted Emotional Wounds
. Our Emotional Defense Mechanisms
. Our Diseases of the Soul/Soul Iniquities (Spots)
. Our Autopilot, Repeating, Neurological Glitches (Wrinkles)
Human Spirit -   **Home of the Holy Spirit**

Can we really reprogram our subconscious mind? The answer is yes, but it is not easy. Part of the difficulty is because we can't see what resides in the innermost part of our soul. We can see the evidence of it by our words and actions, but we can't see the roots.

If we glance through the graphic, we see both the positive and negative parts of our subconscious mind. We can get a better understanding of the human psyche if we use the analogy of a computer.

Our spirit is like a motherboard. Our subconscious mind is like a hard drive. Our conscious mind is like a monitor. And words are a keyboard.

We can't see everything that is on a hard drive. It stores all our data, programs, pictures, and files. A monitor allows us to see some of the programs we have stored on our hard drive. It is a workspace that we can do calculations and create content. Just because we can see information on a monitor doesn't mean that information is stored on the hard drive. We can view internet content on our monitor screen, but the internet content is not downloaded on our hard drive. Likewise, we can hear a great teaching at church but that doesn't mean that information has been saved and downloaded to our subconscious mind.

Neuroscience tells us that we can train our brain. We can reprogram wrong beliefs and behaviors in our subconscious mind and our conscious mind is the gateway. Just like we would use the keyboard and monitor to reprogram a computer, we can use our words and conscious mind to reprogram our sub-conscious mind. Words can reprogram us. The Bible tells us in Romans 10:17 that *"faith comes by hearing and hearing by the word of God."* The word of God, whether that be the written word (logos, the Bible) or the Holy Spirit's spoken word (Rhema), can reprogram our subconscious mind. It can change our identity and change what we believe about ourselves.

As we delve into self-sabotage, recognize that our self-destructive attitudes and actions are rooted in our subconscious mind. As the book explores five major root causes of self-sabotage, please refer back to this chapter as a reference so your understanding can be strengthened.

Chapter 3

The Power of Faith

We need to understand what faith is because having faith in our gut can help override self-sabotaging forces. Surprisingly, most people really don't understand what faith is. I didn't understand it until I was in Bible school. In that five-year period, between 1995 and 2000, when God was teaching me about the human soul, I grew to understand it considerably more.

In its simplest definition, faith is believing, right? While it is true, it isn't true that what we believe in our mind is faith. There are really two kinds of beliefs. There is what we believe in our conscious mind, and there is what we believe in our subconscious mind. True faith is the latter. True faith is what we believe in our subconscious mind.

Remember, we would have a greater level of understanding if we substituted the word "heart" for "subconscious mind" as we read. Faith is what we believe in our heart (subconscious mind) not what we agree with in our mind.

Most Christians haven't caught the revelation that our subconscious mind can be a miracle factory. Mark 11:23 says, *"For assuredly, I say to you, whoever says to this mountain, 'Be removed and be cast into the sea and does not doubt in his heart but believes that those things he says will come to pass, he will have whatever he says."*

Most people don't catch the revelation of this verse because they don't think the verse is true. Perhaps they have spoken to their mountain at different seasons in their life and didn't see any movement. So, while they appreciate the verse being in the Bible because it does offer them hope, most people don't really believe it is true. They haven't understood the *"does not doubt in his heart"* part. Most people have mental agreement with Bible promises, but that is very different than believing them in their heart (subconscious mind). Remember, the subconscious mind is like a hard drive. We can't see what is in it. Just because we see something and agree with it on our monitor doesn't mean it is downloaded on our hard drive. True faith, faith that has the ability to change a current reality, must be present in our subconscious mind.

No other species on the planet has this amazing gift that God gave us. Think about it. God has given mankind the ability to create miracles. Mark 11:23 proves it. Jesus is telling us that mountains can actually move if we have faith for it in our heart. Christians have untapped power. Luke 24:49 talks about being *"endued with power when we receive the Holy Spirit."* Acts 1:8 says, *"But you shall receive power when the Holy Spirit has come upon you; and you shall be witnesses of Me in Jerusalem, and in all Judea and Samaria, and to the end of the Earth."*

Is it any wonder why the devil has worked overtime to try to keep people ignorant and emotionally wounded? When our subconscious mind is wounded, weak, or diseased, we will often reject true faith so miracles can't develop.

Faith is a belief in your subconscious mind for a specific thing. You can have faith in a promise from God or you can have faith that a negative thing will happen. If you believe you will fail, you will fail because your faith is manifesting that reality. Faith has power. Positive faith can move a mountain out of the way or negative faith can move a mountain in your way.

No Fear

How do we know if we have faith for something

imbedded in our subconscious mind or if it is just mental agreement in our conscious mind? We can tell if we have fear.

In the summer of 1996, I was sitting in the West Coast Believer's Convention in Anaheim, California listening to Jerry Savelle preach. At that season of my life, I hadn't made any money in over two years. (It was right before I started working at Coldwell Banker Real Estate). I had attended a Bible School for a year and then after that, I felt like I had a *red light* every time I considered getting a job. It was a very uncomfortable season, but God was teaching me how to trust and obey Him. That day, I had put my very last dollar bill in the offering bucket. I didn't know how I was going to pay the $6 parking fee for the next day. Jerry Savelle was preaching a message that said, "When you are at the end of your rope, let go."

Suddenly, I got it. It was like a light switch flipped on. Fear, anxiety, and pressure over finances was gone. There was a tangle change. Suddenly, I just had peace. That fearless peace was a sign that faith for finances was attached in my subconscious mind.

I somehow had the money for parking the next day and God met my financial needs until I got my first real estate commission about four months later. By the summer of 1996, it had been more than two years since I had left the Fortune 500 computer manufacturer. My severance package only lasted about six months. God supernaturally sustained me financially without government financial aid or family loans. I was late on rent a few times but somehow, I never got evicted. God always made a way.

Sometimes, we don't learn a lesson until we live through it. I know firsthand that God is faithful if we just walk in simple obedience. God trained me how to trust Him with finances. Since then, I have been in seasons of super abundance and super lack. As Paul said, "I know how to abase and abound." But it doesn't faze me. I don't panic if I run short on funds. I walk in obedience on projects even when I don't know where the money will come from.

Faith for Healing

In 1998, I had a raging, infected, abscessed root canal. I had gone to the dentist, and he told me it would cost me $1,400 for a root canal and crown. I didn't have it. I was between real estate transactions, and I only got paid when a property closed escrow. I asked the dentist for antibiotics. He gave me a prescription but told me it wouldn't get rid of the infection. He said it will make the pain subside but as soon as the antibiotics were gone, the pain will return. I was attending the second Bible School at that time. I was scheduled to preach a sermon for my homiletics class, and I just wanted the pain to diminish enough so I could get through my sermon.

It was just as the dentist had said. The pain died down and I was able to give my sermon. As soon as the prescription was done, the pain returned.

I had been journaling that week and it was surprising how many negative thoughts crossed my mind. When fighting a spiritual battle or trying to find your faith, we must get in the habit of taking every thought captive as it says in 2 Corinthians 10:4-5. The passage reads, *"For the weapons of our warfare are not carnal but mighty in God for pulling down strongholds, casting down arguments and every high thing that exalts itself against the knowledge of God, bringing every thought into captivity to the obedience of Christ."*

The verse is telling us that we are to cast down arguments and bring every thought into captivity. That means we need to pay attention to the thoughts that cross our mind. We need to recognize the ungodly ones and respond back with what God says about the situation. I did that when I had the abscessed jaw and below is the *argument*.

"You're not healed"

I countered back, "Yes, I am. By Jesus' stripes I am healed."

"You're not healed. The abscess is going to send you to the hospital with toxic poisoning."

"No, Isaiah 53 says, "Surely, He has borne our griefs and carried our sorrows and by His stripes we are healed. And griefs mean sickness and sorrows means pains. I am healed."

"It's going to cause you to lose some of your teeth."

"No, I'm not going to lose any teeth. Song of

Solomon 4 says, 'your teeth are like a flock of shorn sheep..and none is barren among them."

"Toxic poisoning will get in your blood stream, and you will die."

"No, I shall live and declare the works of the Lord (Psalm 118:17)."

In these situations, demonic forces often try to get us in fear and wear us down with constant negative thoughts. And they usually get away with it because most people don't' pay attention to their thoughts.

After the prescription had ended and the pain had returned, I had a conversation with God as I was driving. Because I had been journaling, I thought I was helping to document the mental attacks I was encountering.

I told God, "I will gladly suffer any pain if it helps me get to the next level with you."

I then heard in my spirit, "It's not My will that you are in pain."

I pulled the car over and sat in a parking lot for a few minutes. I was stunned. Did I have a *martyr mentality* blueprint in my subconscious mind? Was I willing to suffer because I somehow felt it made me more spiritual? Jesus suffered for me, so I was trying to suffer for Him as a payback?

Of course, it wasn't God's will for me to be in pain! How many sermons had I heard that taught that very thing? Was that truth just something I knew in my head and not in my heart? I knew it was the Holy Spirit that spoke that to me, so I meditated on that word from God. After a few minutes, I knew I was healed so I started my car and headed out to finish my errand. I felt like I found that revelation I was looking for, that light switch of faith, if you will. Sure enough, an hour later, all the pain and swelling were gone, and it never came back.

Faith begins at the known will of God. If you know something is God's will, it is so much easier to allow that word to sink down into your heart. Even though God has given mankind the ability to use our faith to move mountains, when we know that it is God's will for that mountain to move, it is easier to activate faith.

We can't fake faith. It doesn't work like that. There have been countless Christians that thought they were standing in faith for their healing, and they passed away. They thought they had faith in their gut but in reality, they had hope, not faith. Having hope is absolutely necessary and I will be discussing that in the next chapter, but faith has teeth. Faith has the power to change a current reality. Faith has life. Hope is like a seed. But faith is like a sprouted seed that is growing into a mustard tree. Faith is like an embryo. It is a fertilized egg that has life.

Certainly, God can sovereignly zap someone healed. Or we can even receive healing by the pastor or church elders praying the prayer of faith over us as it says in James 5:13-16. However, all believers have the ability to obtain healing on their own using their own faith.

The challenge becomes getting the healing teaching from our head to our heart, where it goes from mental agreement to tangible faith.

If our goal is to receive healing by faith, we must get the word of God in us. We should listen, read, and speak Bible verses and teachings that talk about healing. Remember, hearing Biblical teachings on healing is like the computer programmer sitting down at the keyboard. It's the word of God that has the ability to reprogram our subconscious mind and open our heart enough so that faith can sneak through the cracks and get embedded into our heart.

I have heard several testimonies from people that have received their healing after reading the book, "Christ, the Healer" by F.F. Bosworth. The book is full of different teachings on healing. Each lesson approaches the subject in a little different way or with different scriptures. With that much *faith food*, the chances of us swallowing some of it to get it in our gut, is high.

Faith is Not Denial

In 1999, my sister, Stephanie, had a lot of neck and back pain and as a result she visited the Emergency Room quite often. On one of those visits to E.R., they tested her and discovered her spine was "like Swiss cheese" (according to her doctor). Her bones had holes in them. They discovered the cause of it was breast cancer that had metastasized and spread to her spine. Her left breast had a tumor that was three centimeters long.

Stephanie and I were very close in the late 90's. We saw each other three times a week at church, we went out to eat often, and we spoke on the phone several times a day. After the "Swiss cheese" diagnosis, Stephanie told me that she knew she had a lump in her breast for several years, but she never told anyone about it. I asked her why.

She said she had been standing in faith and she didn't want anyone to know because she didn't want them speaking word curses over her. Since the Bible says, *"death and life are in the power of the tongue"* in Proverbs 18:21, she thought it would empower or somehow authorize that cancer to be in her body. She thought if people talked about it, it would permit the cancer to grow.

It is true that the spirit world operates by agreement. We can authorize calamities in our lives if we agree with the negative thoughts that demons whisper in our ear. Likewise, we can activate angels to work on our behalf if we speak the word of God over our challenging situations. There is truth in what Stephanie believed but she used that belief as an excuse not to deal with the very real fact that she had cancer growing in her body. When you have true faith for healing in your gut, it won't matter what other people say about you. It won't matter if people are planning your funeral or demons are throwing a party thinking they have won. Faith is a force that defeats demons and evil or ignorant words of others.

Denying cancer's right to be in your body is a good thing. Positioning your brain to combat negative thoughts is what we should do. Hey, that is what I did with the abscessed root canal. However, we can't assume that we have faith for healing residing in our subconscious mind just because we are countering the negative thoughts with Bible verses. The mere fact that she feared other people knowing about the lump in her breast was evidence that she wasn't *in faith*.

Faith and fear are opposites. As previously mentioned, there is a fearless peace, a knowing in our heart when authentic faith resides in our subconscious mind over a situation. For some people, they feel like a light switch has been flipped.

Stephanie was diagnosed with stage four breast cancer and her doctor's prognosis was bad. I don't remember the percentages, but they didn't think she would live long. She went through radiation and chemotherapy. She was in a convalescent home for three months. Since her cancer was so advanced, she agreed to be part of a trial for a new cancer chemotherapy drug.

While she was doing everything in the natural to get her healing by cooperating with doctors, she was also doing everything in the spirit to obtain healing. She was reading books and listening to preaching tapes. She was in church every time the doors were open, even when I had to bring her in a wheelchair.

There was a point in time where she said she was healed. She said she had a knowing on the inside, but her doctor wouldn't re-test her until after she finished the round of chemotherapy. She obeyed her doctor and finished the chemo. When they finally tested her, all cancer markers were negative. Not only was the tumor gone and all bloodwork was normal but the missing bone in her spine was completely restored. The doctor said her spine looked like a different spine. Her neck and back were completely normal. Stephanie's doctor agreed that this was a miracle.

Stephanie was thrilled. She told everyone she knew that God healed her. She resumed working as a contract administrator at Boeing. She jumped right back to being a workaholic, working 12-hour days.

Her victory was short-lived. One spring day in 2001, Stephanie and I were in the bathroom at a department store. She came out of the stall and lifted up her shirt. One breast was significantly larger than the other. It had sores on it, and it leaked liquid.

A risk of the experimental chemotherapy she had taken was that it could cause cancer. It is believed, even by her doctor at the time, that Stephanie developed an entirely different type of cancer that was caused by the chemotherapy she had taken. This cancer was liquid based and it caused her left breast, leg, and arm to be more swollen than her right side.

At one point, when she had trouble breathing, she went to E.R.. They admitted her and ended up draining two bags full of liquid from her lungs. I was with her that day. The bags of liquid looked like Ziplock bags of chicken noodle soup. It was so gross!

In October of 2001, I was in Hawaii when she started having trouble breathing again. She was scheduled to give a big presentation at work that Monday morning with the V.P. of Boeing. She didn't want to go to E.R. to get her lungs drained because she knew they would admit her for a few days, and she would miss the meeting.

I had wanted to treat Stephanie to a vacation to Hawaii because she was working too hard. But she refused to go because she had that important meeting scheduled so I took a friend instead. I didn't know she was having problems breathing again while I was in Hawaii, but she mentioned it to someone at the Saturday night service at church. I flew into the Orange County airport Tuesday morning and my office at that time was across the street from the airport. I had been at my office less than a half hour, when my secretary told me Stephanie's work was on the phone. The woman on the other end told me that Stephanie never showed up to work for the meeting on Monday and they were concerned. I drove out to her apartment and found her body. Her oxygen level had gotten too low because of the fluid in her lungs. She passed away sometime Saturday night or Sunday.

Stephanie wasn't sure if her healing from the first cancer was because of her faith or if she received it in a prayer line at church. But I want to make this point. You can have faith for finances but not for healing.

You can have faith for cancer but not for diabetes. You can even have faith for one cancer battle but not for a different cancer a year and a half later. Usually, faith for healing is for a targeted ailment.

With Stephanie returning to her 12-hour days of being a workaholic, she wasn't listening to healing scriptures anymore. Her whole focus on life in that season was on her work and that may be why she lost the battle with the second type of cancer.

I recognize Stephanie's story is a little dramatic, but I encourage you to allow it to be a teaching opportunity to recognize the difference between faith and denial. Stephanie was in denial about the lump in her breast for years. If she had gotten medical attention early on, it wouldn't have developed into stage four cancer and would have been easier to treat.

Regardless, real faith is a knowing in your heart. There is peace attached to it. Denial is just hope pretending to be faith. Just because we don't want something to be true, we can't wish it away by refusing to acknowledge that it exists.

Redemptive Promises verses Destiny Promises

Another way to recognize if you have faith for healing in your subconscious mind or not is to check to see if you are healed yet. Faith for healing doesn't take a year to manifest. When there is faith, the healing is either instant or the healing process is accelerated. Destiny promises usually have a gestation period but redemptive promises do not.

Redemptive promises are the promises that Christ came to bring at Calvary. The Greek word for salvation is *sozo*. It means salvation, healing, peace, deliverance, restoration, provision, and prosperity. It means wholeness, nothing broken, nothing missing. When Jesus won the victory on the cross and brought back the keys to the kingdom, He brought back salvation (sozo) and that is available to us.

When we are born again, that salvation comes as soon as it is received and believed in our heart. Likewise, God's peace over a situation can come as soon as it is believed and received in our heart. With provision, someone may not run up to us with an envelope full of cash. But that provision has been released to us and is on the way when we have faith for it in our subconscious mind.

Destiny promises where God tells us aspects of our calling, may take years to manifest. God told Moses he was going to be a deliverer. But Moses killed an Egyptian and spent 40 years in the wilderness before that destiny promise manifested. God gave Joseph dreams, telling him he will be a great leader, but he got sold into slavery and ended up in prison for 14 years before that promise came to fruition. So, if you are standing *in faith* for something, consider which type of promise it is.

It's Human Nature

It has been my observation that most people don't attempt to use faith unless they are dealing with something major or life-threatening. We, as human beings, will tolerate almost anything. We tolerate diabetes, viruses, headaches, tendonitis, nail fungus and most other nuance ailments without even the thought of attempting to fight it with faith. I get it. We are too busy fighting other challenges. We don't mess with the little stuff. Why should we when there are medical treatments for them?

We do the same with financial setbacks. We tolerate mechanical issues with the car, slab leaks at our house, computers malfunctions, and lay-offs at work. We don't try to get God's promises in our gut for health and wealth.

The problem with tolerating ailments and financial challenges is we condition our brain to accept all the trauma and drama the devil may send our way. Neurological pathways are established in our brains to always accept and deal with our problems. We don't get mad enough at the devil to use our faith when challenges come our way.

John 10:10 says, *"The thief does not come except to steal, and to kill, and to destroy. I have come that they may have life, and that they may have it abundantly."* This is Jesus speaking. He is telling us that the forces of evil are assigned to steal, kill, and destroy. If we really believed that our financial lack or nuance medical ailments were the results of demonic attacks, would we do anything about them? The answer to that question is "no" for most people. We authorize calamities in our lives because we attribute them to our own weakness, failures, or genetics. While our failures and genetics may play a role, that doesn't mean the issue wasn't designed by dark forces to attack us.

Faith Can Overrule Self-Sabotage

We all have self-sabotaging blueprints in our subconscious mind and this book will discuss five root causes of them. However, faith is like yeast that can change the whole loaf. If our faith is strong, it can not only move a mountain, but it can also overpower our self-sabotaging tendencies.

Authentic faith has action attached to it as well. We have talked about the peace element, but we haven't talked about the action component.

James 2:18 says, *"But someone will say, 'You have faith, and I have works.' Show me your faith without your works, and I will show you my faith by my works."* James 2:30 says, *"O foolish man, that faith without works is dead."*

Our beliefs and behaviors are driven from our subconscious mind so, of course, what we believe will be demonstrated in our speech and actions. Our faith will drive us to take actions even if it means our fear and other sabotaging forces have to take a backseat. So, in this journey to break self-sabotage, it's important to build our faith at the same time.

We have tremendous potential. 2 Peter 1:3-4 says, *"As His divine power has given us all things that pertain to life and godliness, through the knowledge of Him who called us by glory and virtue, by which have been given to us exceedingly great and precious promises, that through these you may be partakers of the divine nature, having escaped the corruption that is in the world through lust."*

He has given us all things! – past tense. He's not going to equip us. He has equipped us because He gave us a subconscious mind that has the ability to create miracles. What are His great and precious promises? They are the scriptures that talk about healing, prosperity, peace, redemption, and victory. Those scriptures can act like programming codes. Mark 11:23 is a great and precious promise. Jesus authorized us to supernaturally move mountains by us simply commanding it and believing it. He has given those promises and if we just believe them in our heart, we will have them.

Chapter 4

Deposits of Hope

I have been thinking about hope for the last few weeks and I've discovered some interesting nuances. We always talk about faith, but nobody really talks about hope and its importance. The lack of hope is the first of five self-sabotaging root causes I will address in this book.

Our attitude towards hope can be a little hostile. For the most part, we don't want to hope for something because we don't want to be disappointed if it doesn't happen. Afterall, Proverbs 13:12 tells us, *"Hope deferred makes the heart sick, but when the desire comes, it is a tree of life."* Most of us have experienced significant disappointments when something that we expected didn't come. A large percentage of disappointed people become cynical and pessimistic. Many people secretly refuse to hope for things because they don't want to experience disappointment.

Why Is Hope Important?

· God wants us to have hope.

Romans 15:13 says, *"Now may the God of hope fill you with all joy and peace in believing, that you may abound in hope by the power of the Holy Spirit.* This verse tells us that God is a God of hope. He wants us filled with joy and peace and He wants us to believe. He wants us to abound in hope by the power of the Holy Spirit, meaning the Holy Spirit will help us cling to hope.

1 Peter 1:3 says, *"Blessed be the God and Father of our Lord Jesus Christ, who according to His abundant mercy has begotten us again to a living hope through the resurrection of Jesus Christ from the dead."* The word *begotten* means to give birth to or give rise to or bring out. This verse suggests that it is God who births a living hope in us. Because of Jesus' resurrection from the dead, anything is possible, and we need to believe for the impossible.

Jeremiah 29:11 says, *"For I know the thoughts that I think towards you, says the Lord, thoughts of peace and not of evil, to give you a future and a hope."* God's intentions towards us are good. He's not out to get us or punish us. He doesn't set traps to catch us failing in our spiritual walk. He wants us to have a bright future and He wants us to hope and expect that bright future.

· We can't have faith without hope first.

Certainly, we can have hope in our conscious mind for something. We are aware of the things we hope for. However, hope deposits also dwell in our subconscious mind. Hope, like faith, resides in the unseen realm. Romans 8:24 says, *"For we were saved in this hope, but hope that is seen is not hope; for why does one still hope for what he sees?"* In the last chapter, I used the analogy of hope being like a seed and faith being like a sprouted seed, where that seemingly dead seed, now has new life growing.

Hebrews 11:1 says, *"Now faith is the substance of things hoped for, the evidence of things not seen."* Faith is the substance of things hoped for, meaning the substance of faith is birthed out of what we hope for in our subconscious mind. We have to have hope deposits in our subconscious mind before those deposits can get converted to living faith. Hope comes first. Just like there needs to be an egg from the mother before conception can take place, the same is true with faith. There needs to be hope first before the miracle of life, faith, can happen.

· Hopelessness causes depression.

When I was writing the book on depression and suicide (The Suicide Snare), I learned that depression happens when hope is void in a person's life. Depressed people feel hopeless. They don't believe their situation will get better. They don't just snap out of hopelessness by being told, "everything will be okay." They don't believe it. Hope has to be sparked or rekindled. That is why it often takes a spiritual encounter to break depression because hope needs to be infused into the person's heart again.

· Hope strengthens us.

Isaiah 40:1-3 says, *"Comfort, yes, comfort My people!" says your God, Speak comfort to Jerusalem, and cry out to her that her warfare is ended, that her iniquity is pardoned; for she has received from the Lord's hand double for all her sins."* In this passage, God's direction was to bring comfort and encouragement to the people. The human soul needs encouragement and hope.

In fact, bringing hope was one of the main assignments that Jesus had when He was here on Earth. Luke 4:18 says, *"The Spirit of the Lord is upon Me because He has anointed Me to preach the gospel to the poor, He has sent Me to heal the brokenhearted, to proclaim liberty to the captives and recovery of sight to the blind, to set at liberty those who are oppressed."* Jesus came to preach hope. He came to announce the gospel which means good news. He came to proclaim liberty to the captives. As Christians, it is our job to pick up where Jesus left off and encourage those who lack hope. Our words should speak the good news. We are to proclaim liberty to the captives.

Hope strengths our soul. Isaiah 40:31 says, *"But those who wait on the Lord shall renew their strength; They will mount up with wings like eagles, they shall run and not be weary, they shall walk and not faint."* What does it mean when the verse says *wait on the Lord*? When someone waits for someone, they have a hope and expectation that the person will show up. By cultivating and strengthening that hope in God that He will do what He said He will do, it strengths us. It causes us to persevere and not grow weary. It allows us to rise above our current circumstances and believe for a different outcome.

· Hope makes us open to opportunities.

An old quote from Oral Roberts was, "Miracles are either coming to you or by you every day." There are opportunities around us all the time but if we don't expect them, we won't be open to them. We may walk right by that brown paper bag on the bench with money in it. We won't engage in conversation with the lady in the produce isle at the grocery store even though she could be a potential client for our business. We won't smile back at the good-looking man or woman at Target even though we told our friends that we want to get married.

Oftentimes, we use God as an excuse. We tell ourselves that we are waiting on the timing of God for our blessings. When we do that, we remove the responsibility for our success and tell ourselves that our hope is in God to provide. Sure, sometimes that is true. But for most things, God's hand of blessing is on us, but we have to activate it by taking steps towards success. I will dive deeper into expectation in the next section, but in a general sense, our lack of hope is the reason we don't seize opportunities.

Definition of Hope

The definition of hope is: a feeling of expectation and desire for a certain thing to happen. As I have thought about hope the last few weeks, it has dawned on me that a lot people that think they have hope for a certain thing, really don't. They don't have hope for a specific thing in their subconscious mind because they either don't expect it or desire it. It's not real hope if you don't expect or desire it.

Expectation

We can't see the deposits of hope in our subconscious mind, so we don't know if our hope is strong or if it has diminished. A person may have had hope for something years ago and may not be aware that that hope has died out.

- That young couple that hoped for a child, no longer looks at baby clothes and cribs.
- That production manager that attended Bible School 20 years ago, no longer dreams of being a preacher.
- That gas station cashier no longer thinks about starting his own business.
- The waitress with the incredible singing voice, doesn't daydream about making a hit single anymore.
- That PTA mom that had aspirations of being an author, no longer attends writing workshops or tries to design that book cover.
- That 45-year-old single guy that hangs out at the sports bar, no longer thinks about settling down with a nice girl.

It's easy to assume the hope we had a year ago or 20 years ago is still there, but it may have died off. Is the desire still there? Sure, but the expectation isn't. Life happens. We get busy. Or we make assumptions about how something is supposed to happen.

I will give you an example from my own life. At the beginning of last year (2022), I had a few nights where I woke up in the middle of the night and thought about humorous situations in my life. It felt like I was getting ideas for a standup comedy routine. I made notes on the material even though I hadn't done standup comedy in 15 years. I sensed that the Holy Spirit told me that I would have the opportunity to do standup that year.

Shortly after that, I had some medical issues (some negative doctor's reports but I am fine). I got a puppy that demanded a lot of my time and attention. I recorded some YouTube videos. I completed writing two books and got them published. Plus, I worked and cared for my daughter. I got busy and distracted with life or other projects. Completing the books and working was more important than finalizing a five to ten-minute standup routine, especially since there wasn't even a gig scheduled.

My assumption was that if I got asked to do standup comedy, I would have at least a couple weeks to fine-tune the material and memorize it. As the year progressed, my expectation for an invite to do standup decreased, which I was fine with. I am not someone that pines for the spotlight.

In December, I was at a 50th Birthday Party Banquet and they were doing some *open mic* entertainment. I was asked to do some standup comedy there on the spot. I declined because my material wasn't solidified or memorized.

After that happened, the Holy Spirit reminded me that He told me I would have the opportunity to do standup that year. I didn't expect to do standup comedy that night, so I missed the opportunity.

Certainly, a short standup comedy routine isn't a big deal. However, I do believe God wanted to me to share this experience in this book because it is a good example of how we can miss assignments because we don't expect them. If we don't expect the blessing, assignment, or promise, we will miss opportunities as they come to us.

Having an expectation for something means we are equipped and prepared for it. If we still have tasks to do before we are ready, we can sabotage God-ordained opportunities.

We should take an inventory of the things we hope for. Is that hope still alive? Are we prepared for what we are expecting? Have we let the events in life overshadow our goals and assignments?

Desire

To reiterate, the definition of hope is a feeling of expectation and desire for a certain thing to happen. If we were to journal the things we hope for, could we say with all certainty that we desire them?

As a new business owner, would you desire the long hours and hard work? Do you really look forward to obtaining the level of knowledge and training you will need in order to get the business off the ground? As a new parent, do you desire the sleepless nights and cost of a new baby? As an aspiring author, do you really want to learn an industry you know nothing

about? As a new homeowner, do you desire the responsibility of the higher mortgage payment?

All blessings mean more responsibility. Think about
it. The new baby, business, house, and career, all mean
added responsibilities.

We can have hope for things that we may not really
desire. Sometimes, that thing we desire is from God
and other times it is our own vanity. We should examine the things we hope for and ask ourselves some
tough questions.

After we discover that those assignments and
dreams are from God, we should consider our desire
level for those things. Do we really desire that new
blessing to be part of our future? If we don't, we
could be sabotaging opportunities for that new thing
to happen in our lives.

Several years ago, I had dinner with some ladies
from church. One of the women was a nanny and she
was talking about her desire to find a husband. This
woman was a 40-year-old virgin that had never had
a boyfriend. Prior to that evening, I had encouraged
her to try dating sites on the internet to meet some
Christian men. Since she had never been on a date,
I thought it would be a good idea to get comfortable
with dating so she wouldn't be scared or awkward
when she did meet someone who was husband material. She was a good looking, smart woman. I couldn't
see any reason why she was still alone.

At dinner that night, she was telling everyone
about the date she had with a guy she met on a dating

website. She said it was okay until the end of the evening. She said when the guy put his arm around her and leaned in for a kiss, she pushed him away and ran inside the house. Even though it was just a kiss on the cheek, she said it made her feel gross and dirty. I questioned her more about it and we discovered that she had some deep-rooted issues with intimacy and sexuality. Even after marriage, she believed physical intimacy between a husband and a wife was carnal, sinful, and gross. She knew in her head it wasn't, but she had those beliefs in her subconscious mind. There was nothing wrong with her cognitively, but she had the emotional maturity of an eight-year-old. She really didn't want a husband in the traditional sense. She wanted a male best friend that would have a platonic relationship with her, who would provide for her financial needs.

She had a glitch, a wrong blueprint, in her subconscious mind that needed to be corrected. Somehow in her childhood she embraced the idea that human sexuality was bad and dirty, and she never grew out of it. That is not to say that everyone has to have a strong libido, but we shouldn't be repulsed by sex either.

She is currently a Facebook friend. She is still a nanny and is still single without a boyfriend. She thought she was hoping for a husband but because she didn't really desire it, it wasn't real hope. As a result, she pushed away opportunities that may have come her way.

There's Something Else

Sometimes people genuinely have a desire for a husband or wife but they self-sabotage it because there is another situation in their life. They may make excuses, procrastinate, or blame God's timing. But the reason they don't pursue a relationship is, there may be a secret addiction or bad habit they are dealing with. The man may have a pornography or gambling addiction. Maybe the woman is a hoarder or has a shopping addiction. Their logic may be - they will seek a relationship with a future spouse after that *something else* isn't in their life anymore.

The *something else* may not even be something bad. It could be a benchmark a person has set for themselves. The guy may have committed to having a great job or a certain amount in the bank before settling down. The woman could have sworn that she would lose 20 lbs. before allowing herself to date.

I encourage you to journal your thoughts and write down the things you are hoping for. Reflect on your expectation level. Is it still there? Are you prepared if an opportunity presented itself? Do you honestly desire the goal, assignment, or relationship? Be honest with yourself. If you know it is something that God has chartered you to do, ask God to increase your desire. Don't be like my nanny friend. If there are wrong blueprints that are causing wrong beliefs or sabotaging behaviors, work on correcting them.

Expectancy is the Breeding Ground for Miracles

It's easy to get busy with life and not live in an expectant mindset. You know, a big regret I have happened when I attended that second Bible School in 1997 to 1999. The dean of the school of ministry called me in his office and asked me to be the Class President. Wow, what a tremendous honor to be asked. The whole situation caught me by surprise, and I responded in false humility. I said something like, "God has blessed me so much. Maybe we should allow someone else to have this great honor." I wish the dean of the school would have debated with me about it but, instead, he just said, "Okay." I blew it because the opportunity was a surprise to me. That was a large Bible school with hundreds of students, and I messed up.

If we aren't expecting good things to happen to us, we will sabotage the opportunities. Many of us have heard sermons that told us that "expectancy is the breeding ground for miracles." There is a great deal of truth in that statement.

In the mid 2000's, there was a book and movie that came out that taught that we can attract good things to our life by expecting them. The book sold over 30 million copies, so it was a popular concept. It was a little New Age-y so some Christians may not have embraced the phenomenon. The book taught on manifesting things to happen in your life. It talked about visualization, intentions, and mastering your thoughts and feelings.

Even though the concepts were a little too wild for a lot of people, the principles of it were and are in line with Biblical teaching. The Bible tells us to write the vision down in Habakkuk 2:2, which is similar to a vision board. It tells us to "take every thought captive" in 2 Corinthians 10:5 which is similar to mastering your thoughts and feelings. It tells us to renew our mind in Romans 12:2. The Bible tells us to mediate on positive things. Philippians 4:8 tells us, *"Finally, brethren, whatever things are true, whatever things are noble, whatever things are just, whatever things are pure, whatever things are lovely, whatever things are of a good report. If there is any virtue and if there is anything praiseworthy – meditate on these things.*

Expecting good things to happen can work on different levels.

1) It keeps hope alive and active.

2) Actively pursuing a goal can sometimes trigger hope to slip into faith, which will force that goal to happen.

3) We are spirit beings and spirit-beings are carriers of energy. It is possible that our energy may attract what we are expecting.

4) The spirit world operates by agreement so our expectations and words can invite angels or demons into our circumstances.

Destiny Hope Deposits

As previously mentioned, God wants us to have active hope and faith in our heart. When God gives destiny promises, He wants us to have hope for them. God will often give a Rhema promise, vision, or dream to tell us or show us that the vision is His will for our lives. Prior to having the dream or vision, that scenario may not have even been on our radar.

Certainly, Joseph (in the Bible) didn't consider himself a leader and ruler until he had the two dreams that God gave him. In one dream, the sheaves of grain bowed down to him and in the other dream, the sun, moon, and stars bowed down to him. Those dreams planted deposits of hope in him. They branded on his identity that he would be a great leader.

I have heard several preachers say that they saw a vision of themselves preaching and that was one of the ways God called them to ministry. Whether it was in a dream, or a daydream vision, or God illuminating a passage in the Bible, God gives us deposits of destiny hope.

Those destiny hope deposits aren't just for ministry. They could be for businesses, children, special projects, or character traits.

In 1996, when I hadn't worked in over two years, I was reading my Bible and I heard in my spirit, "Covenant Connection Real Estate." I didn't like what I heard. I knew God was telling me He wanted me to start my own real estate company called Covenant Connection Real Estate.

I had gotten my real estate license in 1986 and I attempted to sell real estate then but was not successful. After that, I worked different jobs through a temp agency until one of those temp jobs turned into permanent employment at the Fortune 500 computer manufacturer. I was with that computer manufacturer for six years and I was successful. I started out in a secretarial role and later became the youngest female manager of that 4,000-employee company. I took over a division that had operated in losses and made and saved the company millions of dollars.

But in the summer of 1996, when God gave me the name of the company, I just cringed. Real estate was an area of failure for me. The idea of it brought back bad memories. I knew I couldn't start my own company unless I had my broker's license (instead of just a salesperson license). And I knew I needed to immerse myself back into real estate to re-learn the business.

I sensed God directing me to set up an interview at the local Coldwell Banker Real Estate office near my condo in Irvine. Yuck, yuck, yuck! I was so nervous and uncomfortable going into that interview. I had been a corporate executive, why was I so intimidated by real estate? I don't know why, but God always makes me face my fears. I feared real estate, so, of course, God was going to make me start my own company doing it.

I was with Coldwell Banker until August of 1999, when I left the company to start my own brokerage, Covenant Connection Real Estate. I had gone through the classes for my broker's license and passed the state exam, so I was ready to fulfill God's direction for me.

As mentioned, destiny hope deposits can also be for character traits. We may see ourselves feeding the poor or counseling the discouraged. We may see ourselves giving significant amounts of money to help our church, or we may see ourselves serving our community.

In 1994, after I was enrolled in the first Bible college, I had a couple of action-packed dreams. They were high adventure dreams like *The Raiders of the Lost Ark*. In them, I was like a *Zena, Warrior Princess* where I was fighting demons and winning. I remember thinking after I had the dreams that I didn't have any fear of demons in the dreams.

Then, when I encountered demons in real life, I had zero fear. My heart rate didn't even increase. I describe several of my encounters with demons in my book, *Real Stories of Angels, Demons and the Supernatural.* Most of those demon stories are also on YouTube.

I attribute some of that fearlessness over demonic entities to those dreams. Of course, the fearlessness was strengthened by my experiences. Just like David had the courage to fight Goliath because he fought the lion and bear, the same was true with my demon experiences. I had no fear when I encountered demons either appearing before me or manifesting through a person in the early experiences. So those early experiences gave me the confidence and boldness to remain fearless in some of my later experiences. The dreams partnered with my experiences and branded that characteristic into my identity.

Likewise, when God calls someone to preach, they have the vision or dream God gave them, alongside their preaching experiences, that helps form their identity of being a preacher in their subconscious mind.

It is important to note that when God imprints us with a hope for a calling, business, or project, He gives us a grace and ability to do it. We may not be a *rock star* when we start, but God will use our experiences to teach and train us to be who He has called us to be.

Summary

Remember, hope deposits in our subconscious mind need to have expectancy and desire. If either of those things are weak or missing, we may sabotage opportunities. Expecting something means we are prepared for it.

I encourage you to take an inventory of your hopes. Examine your desire and expectation levels. Are you prepared? Are there tasks you need to do to get prepared? Is there *something else* (bad habit or additional task) that is causing you to procrastinate a specific hope?

Chapter 5

Comfort Zones and Boundaries

A *boundary* is a line that marks the limits of an area, a dividing line. It's a limit of a subject or sphere of activity. And believe it or not, our human psyche has a lot of them. Our comfort zones are those areas that are within our personal boundaries that are established in our subconscious mind.

Comfort zones are the second main root cause of self-sabotaging behavior I will be discussing in this book. Because they reside in our subconscious mind, we may not be aware of them and how they shape our attitudes and decisions.

For some people, the idea of change is terrifying, even if those changes are positive ones. Human nature, unfortunately, will desire and seek out what is familiar to us even though it is not good for us. Why do people stay in abusive relationships? Because what is known is more comfortable than choosing what is not known. The psychological pull of comfort zones is so strong that it will oftentimes sabotage our success.

Friendships

People gravitate towards others that have similar comfort zones and boundaries. A factory worker will seek out others in the same line of work. Why? It's not just because they have their jobs in common. It's because those friends have the same boundaries. None of those factory worker friends have aspirations of becoming a manager, a politician, or an entrepreneur. The friendships are comfortable, and they don't challenge the person to *step up their game*. Their ego feels good around those friends, and they don't feel like they are wasting their life. They don't have anyone telling them or showing them that they are not living up to their potential.

Income

When we are used to struggling financially and

sudden success starts to take us to a new financial level, our comfort zone will often cause us to sabotage our financial success. If we are close to our income boundary, we may start showing up late to our job, or our performance may be substandard, or we may get into unnecessary disputes. Without it even registering in our conscious mind, we could be messing up at work to keep us from succeeding and excelling on the job.

When companies look for new sales representatives, they often look for very successful salespeople, even if that person comes from a different industry. The company may overlook current employees that know the product inside and out and hire someone that knows nothing about the product or industry. Why? Because new employees can learn about products and industries, but you can't teach financial boundaries. Someone that is used to making $150,000 a year will usually gravitate to that income again at the new company. A production operator that makes $50,000 a year would have a difficult time generating enough sales to venture far past his old salary. Even though he would desire $150,000 a year, that income is beyond his current comfort zone so he would most likely sabotage transactions that would cause him to excel on the job.

Housing

I have had clients that settled for an average home,

even when they could have purchased a much more expensive one. They qualified for the more expensive house, but they talked themselves out of it saying the payments were too high. I understand not living beyond your means, but the upscale home was within their means. I'm sure they didn't realize it, but the nice house was outside of their comfort zone. Even with the different reasons they told themselves, the comfort zone thing played a huge role in the house they chose.

In the 90's, I helped a very good friend of mine buy a three-bedroom condo for $120,000 in a city in Los Angeles that bordered Orange County, California. She lived there for about a year and then decided to sell it. I didn't understand why she sold it because she got a great deal on it at the time. When I talked to her about it, she said she just didn't feel comfortable owning her own place. She said she and her family had always been renters. No one in her family had ever owned property and it "just didn't feel right."

As a real estate broker, I have also observed that clients comfort zones not only affect the price range of the houses they buy but their comfort zones also impact the location and features of the home. I have witnessed buyers love ugly houses because it reminded them of the house they grew up in. I have also seen them pick a house in an area known for higher crime rates just because it was their *old stomping grounds*.

Housekeeping

Have you ever noticed that some people are more comfortable with a little clutter while others aren't. My teenage daughter is like that. If her room is clean, within a day, there will be clothes on the floor and her nightstand will have trash on it. Even though there is a trash can in her room, her nightstand will always have several half-filled water bottles, used paper plates, and plastic wrappers of whatever sugary snack she brought up to her room.

I used to have a roommate that when she did the dishes, she always left them in the rack. She wouldn't put them away because she said they needed to dry. But two days later, they were still drying, and I would end up putting them away. In the years we lived together, I don't remember her ever putting the dishes away that she cleaned. I assume that is how she grew up and that is what is comfortable for her.

However, for the people that grew up with the counters cleared or had a consistent habit of putting the dishes away, my friend's behavior would bug them to no end. They wouldn't be able to fully enjoy their TV program in the den because those dishes would be out in plain view.

Weight

I have a tall friend that I have known for more than 20 years. Since I have known her, her weight has fluctuated been between 210 lbs. and 275 lbs. She has weighed 210 lbs. a couple of times but never under it. A couple of years ago, she had weight loss surgery. After her surgery, she got down to 210 lbs. and she currently vacillates between 210 and 225 lbs. Why did she stop losing weight at 210 lbs.? She would look great at 180 lbs. She stopped at 210 lbs. because that was the lowest weight in her comfort zone. If she tried to push lower than 210 lbs., her body, her flesh nature, would fight her with self-sabotaging behavior. I would dare to venture that she won't dip below 210 lbs. until she is able to get a new picture of herself at a lower weight branded into her subconscious mind. For her, the key to weighing under 210 lbs., would be to correct her internal borders (comfort zones) that are established in her subconscious mind.

There is nothing unique about my friend with the 210 lbs. plateau. Most of us have weight ranges embedded into our subconscious mind. Look at young women who get pregnant while they are thin. The majority of them bounce back to their pre-baby weight soon after they give birth. Why? Do they have special bodies with special metabolisms? Usually not. The reason most of them go back to their pre-baby weight right away is, their internal comfort zone drives their weight loss. They don't feel like themselves at the heavier weights and that discomfort pushes them to lose their baby weight. Of course, not all thin people stay thin after having a baby. Some of them have more flexible internal boundaries so their comfort zone makes adjustments to accommodate the higher weight.

Even in my own experience, I have been challenged with my internal weight comfort zones. I remember several times when I was at the low end of my weight border, and I would do something to sabotage my weight loss. I wouldn't even be hungry, and I would grab a snack late at night and devour it. When I was doing it, I thought to myself, "Why am I doing this? It feels like my body is on autopilot."

Certainly, a person can have medical or psychological reasons for carrying extra weight. But our subconscious comfort zones can play a big role in self-sabotaging weight loss.

Dating

In dating scenarios, it is common for both men and women to sabotage and limit their relationships because of their fear of authentic intimacy. Fear of transparency and vulnerability has caused many single people to walk away from relationships they shouldn't have left. It's not comfortable to feel vulnerable so our walls go up and we sabotage the momentum of the relationship.

Our Boundaries

Proverbs 4:23 says, *"Keep your heart will all diligence, for out of it spring the issues of life.* The word *issues* is the Hebrew word *totsa'ah*, which is also translated as *boundaries*. So, this verse encourages us to work on our subconscious mind because from it springs the boundaries of our life.

Our comfort zone boundaries can be expanded. Whenever I think about comfort zone boundaries, Isaiah 54:2-3 comes to mind. The passage reads, *"Enlarge the place of your tent, and let them stretch out the curtains of your dwelling; do not spare; lengthen your cords, and strength your stakes, for you shall expand to the right and to the left, and your descendants will inherit the nations."*

There are three effective ways to combat comfort zone boundaries:

- Recognize our boundaries. Proverbs 4:23 says, *"Keep our heart with all diligence..."* The word *diligence* means to persistently work on. So, this verse encourages us to persistently work on identifying and understanding our subconscious boundaries. Journal the limitations we have subconsciously put on ourselves. Why have we limited ourselves? How can we break that limitation off of us?
- When it comes to comfort zone fears, the best way to fight it is to do it afraid. If public speaking is way outside our comfort zone, we should make ourselves do it. If dating is outside of our comfort zone, join a dating site and make ourselves

meet new people. If going back to school is uncomfortable, we should force ourselves do it. We shouldn't allow excuses and procrastination to stop us from making tangible steps forward.

- Ask God to help us. The Holy Spirit can tell us if we are self-sabotaging because of subconscious limitations. Also, God can tell us if the task we are focused on is His will for our life or not. When a goal is something that God wants us to do, it's a lot easier to step out of our comfort zone to do it. I did not want to step foot into that Coldwell Banker office and go back into real estate. But it was a matter of obedience, so I had to override my comfort zone and do it. God will help us. We need to lean into Him, and we will be surprised how far we can reach.

Chapter 6

Recognizing Self Blame

Unforgiveness towards ourselves is the third root cause of self-sabotage discussed in this book. We may not even be aware that we are harboring offense towards ourselves but that doesn't mean that we aren't subconsciously punishing ourselves for our past mistakes.

Several years ago, when I was an altar worker at a large church, there was a young woman that had come through the prayer line that I prayed for. Later in the counseling room, she told me that she cut herself and she showed me her arms that had fresh wounds and old scars.

She proceeded to tell me that when she was a little girl, she was in the yard with her father who was doing yard work. She climbed on the roof of the shed and jumped off, landing on their dog. She had seen western movies where the cowboy jumped off a roof and onto his horse, and she was trying to do the same thing with her dog. When the girl landed on the dog, it broke the dog's leg.

The father screamed at the little girl and told her that they had to kill the dog to put it out of its misery. The father got a knife and slit the dog's throat and made the little girl watch. He then took the little girl's head and rubbed her face in the dog's blood.

That little girl, who had become a young woman, hadn't forgiven herself. Rather than recognizing that that traumatic event was her father's fault, she carried the burden of guilt. That event emotionally scarred her in a huge way. Because she blamed herself, a sub-conscious blueprint was established that told her to punish herself. She cut herself to punish herself. She probably did other self-sabotaging and harmful things to herself, but I lost contact with her, so I don't know.

That girl's experience was so horrible, it's hard to imagine. However, it is a good example of what we can do in our own lives. We can take a situation from the past and blame ourselves for it. We can point to one aspect of a situation and embrace complete blame for something terrible. Yes, the little girl shouldn't have jumped on the dog. She did it in ignorance. But a good, normal father would have just taken the dog to the vet. The father's ignorance and anger were the real villains in the story.

Like the girl in this story, maybe we are blaming ourselves for a situation where we were just one component of the story, and not the main reason for the tragedy. Believe it or not, misappropriating blame is extremely common. And when a person carries blame, they often subconsciously self-sabotage to punish themselves.

The Blame Game

I have talked about the boyfriend I had that committed suicide in my books *The Suicide Snare* and *Real Stories of Angels, Demons, and the Supernatural*. If you haven't read those books and aren't aware of my past, I will share a little about that experience because it can help bring an understanding about dissecting blame.

I am not going to go into all the details of that experience in this book, but I encourage you to read about it in one of the books I just mentioned. There are a lot of very interesting details that may shock you.

Being Fred's girlfriend was like being on a roller-coaster. There would be a lot of highs and lows. He was bipolar. He would be wonderful, charismatic, and loving for three weeks a month. And then be withdrawn and indifferent for a week until he snapped out of it. In the two years I dated him, it wasn't uncommon for him to break up with me and then beg me to reconcile a week later.

I had told Fred that the next time he broke up with me, that would be it. I wouldn't reconcile again. Well, in January of 1993, Fred broke up with me. Sure enough, a couple weeks later he wanted to get back together again. He tried several times, but I was done. I was always gracious and kind to him when he reached out to reconcile but I told him I couldn't.

He ended up shooting himself through the heart exactly two years to the day that we had started dating. I will mention this, he did leave me a *goodbye* cassette tape. He was very nice and loving on the tape saying I wasn't the reason for his decision. He said he had been on that collision course with himself all his life. He also said on the tape that he remembered what I had told him about God. He said he was going to ask Jesus into his heart and make peace with God before he takes his life.

At the funeral, Fred's sister read a paragraph out of his journal where he said if he couldn't make it work with me, he couldn't make it work with anyone. His line of thinking was that I was his last chance at finding love. Well, his sister read that and insinuated that I was to blame for his suicide. She even implied that I had a lot of nerve to show up at the funeral.

I wasn't a scheduled speaker, but when my friend, Sharon, got up to give the eulogy, she said I could go up with her. After Sharon finished, I told the 200 people there about the angel that appeared to Sharon's husband, Darryl. The angel told him, "Fred is dead but he is with the Lord." I also told them about the audio tape that Fred left me and that he said he was going to ask Jesus into his heart. And then I preached salvation to the audience.

I didn't take on the blame that his sister tried to put on me. I knew there were several factors that contributed to Fred's state of mind. Even then, I knew how to appropriate blame. There were four factors that played a role in Fred's decision to take his life.

1) Yes, he wanted to reconcile our relationship and I didn't want to. But this wasn't a teenager dealing with his first love. Fred was a 36-year-old divorced man. He had had a handful of other girlfriends in his life. It wasn't like our relationship was an all-consuming love story. What bothered him about our break-up was, he had bought into the lie that said, "if he couldn't make it work with me, he couldn't make it work with any-one." I have an easy-going personality and I am easy to get along with. But I wasn't his perfect woman; and I wasn't his soulmate. If he had learned how to break that emotional rollercoaster thing, he could have made someone a wonderful husband. All that aside, he did love me, and he felt he made a mistake by breaking up with me again.

2) Another huge factor in his suicide was his

relationship with his father. He hated his father because his father was a drunk all his life. During the time that we were dating, Fred started to see a psychiatrist and he had some repressed memories resurface. Fred remembered that he was forced to live with his father when he was 13 years old after his parents divorced. He remembered some of his father's drunken episodes and he remembered being sexually abused by his father on several occasions.

Fred had a very difficult time emotionally processing that discovery. Also, I think the psychiatrist kept pushing him to question his own sexuality. Could the reason he kept breaking up with the women in his life be that he may be gay? I think the psychiatrist was trying to force him to consider that possibility. That wasn't something that Fred wanted to consider. I can say with all confidence that I don't think he experimented sexually as an adult. But it was possible that he could have had unexplored bi-sexual tendencies. At that time, in the early 90's, people with bi or fluid sexuality were told they were lying to themselves. The culture, at that time, refused to accept bisexuality. Bisexuals were told that they were gay, but they just hadn't fully accepted it yet. Today that viewpoint has changed. Bisexual tendencies and fluid sexuality is accepted in our culture. However, the fact that he went along with his father's sexual abuse made him question his sexuality and his whole identity.

I think that is the real reason he broke up with me on that January morning in 1993. I think he was bombarded with new information and new questions, and he needed some time and space to figure it out.

3) Another issue that tormented him was his debt. He had anxiety and he would stew and worry about debt. His debt was under $3,000, yet to him, it may as well have been a million dollars. He would think about and talk about his debt way too much. He had a good, steady job and made decent money. However, the whole idea of owing money to a bank terrified him. A little molehill of debt felt like a huge mountain to him. It consumed his peace. Those quiet moments that should have been filled with blissful relaxation, were instead times of rehearsing how and when he could pay back that debt. He wouldn't let himself have peace; instead, he rehearsed negative, fearful thoughts.

4) The fourth factor in his suicide was his medication. His psychiatrist had Fred on Prozac which is a regular anti-depressant. Fred was clearly bi-polar which was evidenced by his mood cycles, and he should have been on a bi-polar medication. But Fred's psychiatrist thought that since he didn't turn super mean when he was depressed, he wasn't manic-depressive.

Not only was it the wrong medication for his mental issues, but Prozac had side effects. A side effort was a person could have suicidal thoughts if they stopped taking it abruptly. Fred knew that he wasn't supposed to drink alcohol while on Prozac, so when he started drinking when he broke up with me, he stopped taking his medication. His brain chemicals were already out of whack, but discontinuing Prozac cold turkey, sent him into more of a tailspin.

It is a good idea to emotionally process traumatic events in your life. Write out the details in a journal. Recognize your role in the situation. Don't whitewash it and play the victim. But don't embrace the role of the villain either. Put yourself in other people's shoes and try to understand their perspectives so you can see the incident from different angles. It would have been easy to wear the cloak of shame over Fred's death, but there were other factors, and it was ultimately his decision. When we analyze the trauma and drama in our life, it's important to recognize our role in it but we shouldn't go overboard and weigh our role incorrectly.

I was surprised by the number of people that told me after Fred's suicide that they felt responsible for his death. They were experiencing guilty feelings because they said they should have seen the signs.

Several of Fred's friends were bombarded with thoughts of *would have, could have, should have.* Some of them wrongly embraced blame when they shouldn't have. While others tried to deflect blame by blaming others. As a defense mechanism, when a person doesn't know how to appropriate guilt, or consider all the contributing factors, they sometimes will put all the blame on someone else. They do that so their mind doesn't absorb thoughts of self-blame.

Neither accepting full blame nor deflecting blame are emotionally healthy. Situations should be objectively evaluated to make sure all compensating factors are weighed correctly. We don't want to live in delusion. We want to accept responsibility for the things that are our fault and not blame shift to other people or situations. But we also don't want to accept full blame for situations that we only contributed to in a minor way.

What If We Are Guilty?

Most of us have experiences in our past that we regret. However, some of us have sins, mistakes, or other actions in our past that have marked us. Our own foolishness or lapses in good judgment may have caused great harm to others. Some of us may even have subconsciously embraced the idea that we don't deserve forgiveness. It is not uncommon for people to subconsciously sabotage their success in life because of hidden, undiagnosed unforgiveness towards themselves. I have known people that wasted their life living in the regrets of their past.

If we don't forgive ourselves, we are telling God that the sacrifices Jesus made on the cross weren't big enough to cover all our sins. God's grace is sufficient to cover our mess ups. We need to extend the same grace towards ourselves that God does.

If you aren't sure if you are holding unforgiveness towards yourself, reflect on the mistakes, disappointments, or wrong turns you have made. If there is an area of regret, ask God to reveal to you if you are holding unforgiveness towards yourself. If you are, repent of the sin of unforgiveness and ask God to help you fully release it.

We, as Christians, don't get the option to select which sins we get to keep. For some of you reading this book, God is telling you it is time to forgive yourself.

If there is an area of active sin in your life and that is the area that you don't forgive yourself from, then you would obviously need to address the root sin issue first before addressing self-forgiveness. But whatever the area is, know that God stands ready to help you with it.

With that said, too many people are carrying around guilt, regret, shame, and unforgiveness that needs to be released. If God can forgive you, then take His lead and forgive yourself.

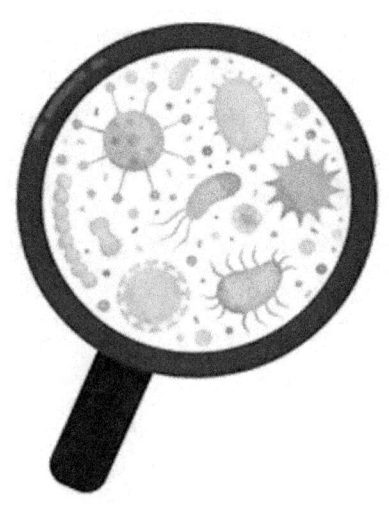

Chapter 7

Diseases of
the Soul

The fourth root cause of self-sabotage that I will be discussing in this book are *Diseases of the soul* (also known as soul iniquities). They are propensities or bents towards certain types of sin. They are our weaknesses, our *pet sins*, our blind spots. They reside in our subconscious mind so a person may or may not be aware that they have that character trait. They act like cancers where they can grow and metastasize without us even knowing that they are silently killing aspects of our life. They can subtly influence our beliefs and behaviors and can sabotage our relationships, finances, careers, and destinies.

They are:
1) pride
2) fear
3) unforgiveness/offense
4) jealousy/envy
5) rebellion
6) religious pride
7) prejudice/hatred
8) weak willpower
9) sexual sins, addictions, and fetishes
10) idolatry
11) greed/selfish ambition
12) negative/critical/judgmental mindsets

A more comprehensive study of them can be found in my books *Blind Spots and Wrinkles* and *Diseases of the Soul*. Those books give a more thorough teaching on soul iniquities, and there is a chapter for each of the 12 soul strongholds listed above. Those books discuss several ways each *disease of the soul* can manifest in our behavior so diagnosing them in our life is easier. But in this chapter, I am going to give a brief overview and then discuss the ones that can cause the most self-sabotage.

One of the biggest misconceptions people have is, when they think of sin, they assume there is always a temptation and people make a choice to do wrong instead of doing what is right. However, with bents towards certain types of sin, a person can make a comment or take an action in almost an auto-pilot manner, and they may not realize that their comment or action was rooted in an iniquity residing in their subconscious mind. A large percentage of the sins committed that are motivated by a person's soul iniquities are auto-pilot responses. They usually are not thoughtfully considered before the person jumps in and acts.

Another misconception is, we don't view our *pet sins* as sins. *Pet sins* are the sins that we have that we are used to and comfortable with. When we make comments or take actions that are rooted in pride, we don't really think we are doing anything wrong. We can certainly justify our actions to ourselves and others. Another example would be, if you had a co-worker that just criticized another employee to you. In her mind she was just making observations and commenting on the perceived flaws of that other employee. She doesn't view her actions as slanderous. She may be clueless that her assassination of that co-worker's character could be based out of jealousy in her own heart.

Most people have three or four *diseases of the*

soul residing in their subconscious mind; however, the broader range is between two and six of them. If the average Christian looks at the list of the 12 *diseases of the soul*, they may pick out a couple of them that they think they have. However, a significant percentage of people have soul iniquities that they are unaware of.

There is a lady I have known for a couple of years and by my observation, she has at least eight soul iniquities. I have never met anyone besides her that had that many. Her soul diseases feed off each other so, needless to say, she is not pleasant to be around. Like most people with a lot of junk in their subconscious mind, she blames everyone else for her emotional wounds and drama that seems to follow her. She doesn't know she is the one causing the hurt and drama.

Pride

Most people don't see pride as that big of a deal. We have been conditioned to believe that pride is good. There are verses in the Bible that tell us that God hates pride. Yet, somehow, our culture doesn't view pride as a bad thing.

In fact, the word *pride* was negative and associated with sin until the 14th century when a positive connotation started to be associated with the word. Pride took on a whole new meaning, and the word began to be known as an emotional response or attitude of self-respect. The word *pride* is now associated with self-esteem, dignity, and honor.

According to Merriam-Webster, "Pride is a word that has had a number of changing meanings over its lifetime." I believe this may have been intentional. The kingdom of darkness may have orchestrated the change of meaning of the word. Afterall, the Bible tells us that Lucifer was kicked out of heaven because of pride. So, of course, it would be a good idea to whitewash his sin and make it seem like God over-reacted.

Pride is at the base of all *diseases of the soul*. When I envision pride in our subconscious mind, I don't see it as one spot like the other soul iniquities. I see it more like a giant spiderweb or root system that has strings in every corner of our subconscious mind. Our Adamic nature, our human carnality, has pride oozing out of us with almost every sentence. It is so ingrained in us and intrinsic to our existence that we don't notice it.

With Satan's victory in the Garden of Eden, pride was sired into the blood line of humanity. When Adam and Eve sinned, they immediately hid from God. Hiding sins is a demonstration of pride. Adam and Eve also felt the need to hide their nakedness. Again, hiding, being self-conscious, and being embarrassed are all signs of pride. Carnality in the souls of mankind was birthed at the fall so, of course, humans would carry pride since it was grafted into us at Satan's victory. The children carry what is in the father. And

Father Lucifer had pride so humanity, in our current state, carries pride.

If we take measures to reduce our pride, then it will be much easier to see our other *diseases of the soul* and uproot them. Pride is a major cause of blind spots and when we are blind to certain realities, we will take missteps. We will self-sabotage.

Pride Weakens Discernment

A root of pride in someone's subconscious mind can give them a cold heart. Ezekiel 11:19 and 36:26 both talk about God removing our "heart of stone" and giving us a heart of flesh. Our pride and sinful nature can cause our hearts to harden.

To illustrate it, when we have a strong root of pride in our cold, hard heart, it is like a frozen pond in our soul. If someone were to throw a stone at a frozen pond, most likely that pebble would bounce a few times but wouldn't crack the ice. I envision that metaphorical layer of ice between our conscious mind and our subconscious mind. It is difficult for new information to get in.

Our hard heart can make it very difficult for God's word to sink from our conscious mind down into our subconscious mind. Unless we take measures to uproot pride, we may have a very difficult time receiving authentic faith since faith resides in our subconscious mind.

As well, we won't be open to new information from

other people. A prideful person thinks they know everything they need to know. And whether they verbalize it or not, they believe there isn't anything a peer or subordinate can say to them that would be beneficial to them. A prideful person believes their version of the truth is the real truth, and if anyone disagrees with them, then they are wrong. Pride blinds a person so they can't see their own self-deception.

The hardness of our heart can not only restrict information coming into our conscious mind and subconscious mind, but it can also block information coming from our spirit. The voice of the Holy Spirit that would normally travel from our spirit, through our subconscious mind, and register as a thought in our mind, can get blocked. When our pride causes our heart to be hard and cold, we will have a very difficult time hearing the Holy Spirit's guidance. Our discernment will be flawed and there will be more opportunities to self-sabotage and make wrong decisions.

Pride Leads to Deceptive Thinking

King Nebuchadnezzar refused to turn from his pride, and he went crazy and ate grass for seven years. Both David Koresh and Jim Jones were preachers who started out with correct theology. But they got lifted up in pride, created their own wrong doctrines, and turned their congregations into cults. David Koresh called his followers the *Branch Davidians* and most of them were killed in a gun battle and fire in Waco,

Texas. Jim Jones was going to be exposed by a journalist and a politician, so he had them killed. He then orchestrated a mass murder-suicide by compelling his followers to drink poisoned Kool-Aid in a commune in Jonestown, Guyana.

Pride is a breeding ground for deception. Luke 1:51-52 says, *"He has shown strength with His arm; He has scattered the proud in the imaginations of their hearts. He has put down the mighty from their thrones, and exalted the lowly."* Pride causes *imaginations of our hearts.* Typically, the more pride a person has, the more delusional their thinking is.

Lucifer is called the *Deceiver,* and when we are lifted up in pride, we give the reigns of our soul over to the enemy to plant all sorts of wrong thinking. I know that sounds a little dramatic, but it is true. Think of the proverbial angel sitting on one shoulder and the devil sitting on the other shoulder in that idiom that dates back to the 16th century. It depicts how the devil tempts us to do wrong, while the angel on the other shoulder encourages us to do good. Since pride can block our discernment to hear from God, it is much easier for demonic suggestions to manipulate our pride and convince us to believe a lie. Layers of deception can cloud our perception of reality to the point that we are living in a false reality. Pride causes a person to believe their version of truth even if the real truth is completely different than their version.

Think about it for a moment. Someone that is extremely prideful is more likely to jump into questionable business ventures. Someone who is prideful will walk away from an important relationship because their ego got a little bruised. Someone who is prideful will lie to *save face* and end up destroying an important project negotiation.

Fear

Fear is the most obvious soul iniquity that we would assume causes self-sabotage. Fear is a liar and a thief. Fear has convinced people to do or not to do so many things. If we stop to consider the affects fear has had on individuals, families, and countries, it would be alarming. Fear has started wars between countries and in families. Fear has ruined the lives of people who have lived in consent worry and anxiety. Fear has even driven some people to suicide or homicide. It has stopped some people from pursuing God-ordained relationships, educational advancements, business opportunities, and inventions. Fear has stolen many blessings that God intended His children to have.

There are five categories of fear. 1) safety fear, 2) comfort zone fear, 3) impending harm fear, 4) fear of evil fear, and 5) the *disease of the soul* fear.

· Safety Fear

I believe this category of fear is really the only good type of fear. We have or we should have an innate fear in us that tells us not to engage in dangerous activities. We shouldn't disturb a hornet's nest. We should fear walking on the ledge of a 20-story building. We should fear swimming with crocodiles. These are not irrational fears; these are normal life-preservation cautionary fears.

· Comfort Zone Fear

A person can be apprehensive of things they are not comfortable with and not have a stronghold of fear in their subconscious mind. Just because someone has a fear of public speaking, doesn't necessarily mean they have the *disease of the soul* of fear.

We addressed comfort zones and boundaries in the last chapter. We understand that it is in our human nature to fear things we are not comfortable with. These kinds of fears don't go away by themselves. They go away when we push ourselves to get out of our comfort zones. We need to stretch ourselves and do the uncomfortable things, so fear doesn't stop us from obeying the assignments that God has for us.

· Impending Harm Fear

This type of fear can happen when we get a negative doctor's report or a phone call at 3:00 am telling us a family member has been in an accident. It is fear that washes over us when we hear bad news.

Fear of impending harm, either for ourselves or our

loved ones, is something that most of us have faced in our life. I know from experience that when we first get a negative doctors report, we are shocked. Sometimes it takes a few days to reconcile the information we just received in our minds. Oftentimes, when we get a negative report, we aren't ready to stand in faith right away because we are still numb from the news. I get it. I have been there more than once.

· Fear of Evil

This type of fear is fear of the kingdom of darkness. It is walking into a dark room and feeling a little nervous. Or it's your heart beating fast because there is a dark shadow in your bedroom. It is fear of demons.

As Christians, we shouldn't fear demons. Demons thrive when fear and ignorance are present. They are like cockroaches; as soon as the light is switched on, they stamper and flee. I highly recommend that Christians learn about the spirit world and know how to cast out demons. Hosea 4:6 says, *"My people perish for lack of knowledge."* If you fear evil, I suggest reading Kenneth Hagin's book, *The Believer's Authority,* and my book, *Real Stories of Angels, Demons, and the Supernatural.*

If people live in fear and ignorance of the spirit world, the kingdom of darkness can wreak havoc in their lives. All Christians should take an active role in dispelling fear and ignorance, so God's will can be done on Earth.

· The *Disease of the Soul* Fear

The final type of fear is the soul iniquity of fear. An iniquity of fear is when that fear is a stronghold in a person's subconscious mind . It is more than comfort zone fears. It isn't a matter of feeling nervous with things you aren't comfortable with. It is a stronger fear that can terrorize and traumatize a person.

"How can we distinguish between comfort zone fears and a *disease of the soul* fear?" Below are some questions you can ask yourself that may help bring clarity:

- Do you have any phobias?
- Are there things that terrify you that don't bother other people?
- *Diseases of the soul* can originate out of a *generational curse*, a demon, or a traumatic event in your past. Is fear a *generational curse*? Do you think you have a demon of fear? Was there an event in your past that may have scarred your psyche and birthed a root of fear in you?
- Has God given you assignments, but you haven't done them because of fear?
- Are there actions you take or don't take that others don't understand?

A person with a soul iniquity will self-sabotage on a daily basis. With every decision rooted in fear, they will absolutely limit any positive opportunity that may come their way. Comfort zone fears can also stop our forward momentum and cause us not to step out when we should.

Unforgiveness/Offense

The soul iniquity of unforgiveness and offense is one of the most common soul diseases people possess. I would estimate that around 75% of people have this dark spot in their soul. That is not to say that the other 25% don't occasionally get emotionally wounded and have a hard time forgiving someone. But the difference is when they release it, they release it. They don't think about it anymore and oftentimes forget the details of the offense over time. I've noticed that people with the *disease of the soul* of unforgiveness don't forget offensive incidents as easily. People in that 25% group, depending on the details of the occurrence, usually forget the issue within hours, days, or weeks. If it was an emotionally traumatic event, they may remember it for a longer period, but the issue isn't something they rehearse in their mind. If they were asked about the offense a year after they forgave the emotional wound, some of the details of emotional wound would be a bit fuzzy in their memory because they hadn't thought about it in a long time. Whereas a person with a root of unforgiveness can usually remember most of the details of the event and then even create some additional fabricated details that strengthen their right to be mad or hurt.

So why would a stronghold of unforgiveness in someone cause them to self-sabotage? Unforgiveness is when you get your feelings hurt or you are offended by somebody. However, it can grow into a spirit of offense the same way cancer grows in different stages. Unforgiveness is like the early stages of cancer and the spirit of offense is like stage 4 cancer. It's the same cancer but just at different levels of advancement. Unforgiveness is a wounded area in the subconscious mind. But when it turns ugly, it becomes a spirit of offense. Offense is the mean side of unforgiveness.

When someone has a spirit of offense, negative attitudes and actions will manifest through them. The disease of offense festers inside them and their thinking becomes a little delusional. They often re-write history in their own minds. Then, they try to convince others of their version of reality. They project wrong motives towards others. They can assume random acquaintances have negative intentions, as well, not just the people they hold offense towards. When offense is a stronghold in a person's subconscious mind, that offense usually links arms with their pride, and they start to believe all kinds of false scenarios. They can even seek revenge and they convince themselves they are entitled to harm that person. They take it upon themselves to play judge and jury over the perceived wrongs of others.

When a person has a stronghold of unforgiveness and offense, they usually self-sabotage and make wrong decisions. They will most likely misjudge the motives of others and mess up opportunities that may come their way.

Jealousy/Envy

Jealousy is another common *disease of the soul.* Those that have the soul iniquity of jealousy assume that everyone has it and that just isn't the case. Jealousy is not like pride; not everyone has it in their subconscious mind. However, of those that carry it, there can be different amounts, levels, or stages of it in different people. One person may have a grape-size black spot of jealousy that rarely manifests. While another person may have a grapefruit-sized ugly, diseased, cancerous tumor of jealousy that ruins relationships and causes the person to be consistently bitter and hostile.

Most people think that jealousy and envy are the same thing. Although the two words are synonymous, there are some slight differences. Envy is the presence of discontentment or ill will at another's good fortune or a dislike for a person who has what they want. Jealousy is a little more layered because there are different types of jealousy. The positive side of jealousy means to guard or protect something or someone. The negative side means either overprotective or envious. The negative side of jealousy is dangerous because a person's thinking can become distorted. Jealousy causes an evil passion to be stirred up in a person's imagination.

Jealousy/envy is an ugly sin, but our culture does not recognize the seriousness of this soul iniquity. In some circles, jealousy is considered a compliment. One woman may say to another, "Your husband is so great; I'm so jealous," or say, "I love your new furniture; I'm so envious." Of course, many in our culture do not recognize it as a bad thing, when it's treated as a casual compliment.

When someone desires what someone else has, they are being short-sighted. They don't know the other person's whole story. They don't know the struggles they faced or the challenges they may have been through. Maybe that person endured endless hours of studying and training to educate themselves so they could afford that car you envy. Were you willing to pay the same price? If you were, there is still time. Improve yourself so you can make more money. Someone else may be jealous of a person's trim body. Well, are they willing to pay the price of dieting and exercise to get a trim body? Recognize that most of the things that people envy came at a price. What they achieved can be accomplished by others that are willing to pay the same price.

Some belongings and features that people may envy are not necessarily things that the person that has them, has earned. Perhaps fortune just smiled on them and blessed them. Maybe a woman just naturally has a pretty face. Well, good for her. Why does that have to affect you? You should be happy for her and not angry with her.

Envy is a breeding ground for evil. James 3:14-16 says, *"But if you have bitter envy and self-seeking in your hearts, do not boast and lie against the truth. This wisdom does not descend from above, but is earthly, sensual, demonic. For where envy and self-seeking exist, confusion and every evil thing are there."*

Contention, strife, and discord thrive when jealousy abounds. In fact, this may surprise you, but out of all the *diseases of the soul*, I consider jealousy to be the most dangerous one for a company, organization, or church. I have had employees with a strong root of jealousy and all they did was bring strife and division to the company. I can usually spot it a mile away. If there is a person that is always gossiping and bringing drama, nine times out of ten, it is because there is a root of jealousy in them. I have been on teams where there was a dozen of us, and I observed nasty cat fights between the women that carried a root of envy. In group dynamic situations, I have watched those with jealousy contend for the position of *queen bee*. The jealous woman would have conversations with others that they weren't threatened by, and they would try to discredit those they deemed as their competition. They would try to sabotage the work of others. Jealous people attempt to point out the flaws of their competition. I have been amazed in situations where a jealous person was extremely kind and generous with the person they envied and then turned around and said evil, vile things against them. I have witnessed a music team at a church completely get dismantled by the drama that a jealous person brought in.

As well, people with jealousy can team up together and accomplish great evil. We can see examples of that in the Bible. Josephs brothers were jealous of him, so they sold him into slavery. The pharisees were jealous of Jesus, so they turned into a murderous mob demanding his death. When jealous people link arms with other jealous people, they tend to feed off each other's energy and a murderous mindset can grow. As a group, they will become more venomous than they would as an individual.

In today's world, a band of jealous people may not show up with pitch forks demanding a person's physical death, but they can certainly assassinate the character of someone. That murderous spirit can destroy a person's career, relationships, or reputation. People with a root of jealousy seem to be drawn to each other like magnets and when they are together, they can do great harm to any group dynamic.

They call jealousy the *green-eyed monster*. Well, that monster will sabotage their relationships, finances, and career opportunities.

Weak Willpower

Self-control is about more than how often we exercise. It involves overcoming addictions, controlling what we say, managing our bodies, our time, and our money. 1 Corinthians 9:27 says, *"But I discipline my body and bring it into subjection, lest, when I have preached to others, I myself should become disqualified."* The word *subjection* means to bring something under dominion or control. It doesn't mean we are legalistic or never eat a donut but rather it means we control our flesh nature, and our flesh nature doesn't control us. Whatever the area is, we have the power to control ourselves and not be a slave to our carnal nature.

None of us are perfect, so does that mean that everyone has a soul iniquity of weak willpower? No. Just because most people have areas of their life where they lack self-discipline, doesn't mean that area is a soul iniquity.

To put it in gardening terms, let's equate these self-control areas to weeds. Most of us have weeds in our front garden. We know we should be more diligent to remove the weeds, but we are busy, and the weeds are not our priority. Weeds are an annoyance, and they can spring up out of nowhere. However, weeds are relatively easy to pull out; we don't need a tractor to uproot them. You, as an individual, can pull them up. However, there are people that don't just have a few little 5-inch-tall weeds; they have weeds that have grown into 5-foot-tall stalks that can't be easily uprooted. The stalks are thick and sturdy, and the person can't pull them out of the ground because the root system is too strong. Those weeds that are 5 feet tall, are the strongholds in our life.

People with those kinds of discipline strongholds

need help. If the issue is obesity, they may turn to weight loss surgery. If the issue is drugs or alcohol, they may seek help from AA, Celebrate Recovery, or even a rehab treatment. The key to diagnosing if a self-discipline area is a soul iniquity or not is, can the person correct it on their own? Has the person tired and failed enough times to admit that it is a stronghold?

When someone lacks discipline, they are usually lazy, and they procrastinate what they should be doing. As a result, they damage their relationships and career.

Negative/Critical/Judgmental Mindset

A soul iniquity of a critical spirit is usually a by-product of one of the other *diseases of the soul*. Someone with a root of pride can also have a critical spot in their subconscious mind. They may have a know-it-all demeaner so, of course, they will criticize any idea or project that they didn't originate. Someone with unforgiveness/offense will look for opportunities to criticize and judge the person that they hold in derision. Or it can be a byproduct of religious pride, rebellion, jealousy, prejudice, or fear.

While a critical spirit can be a byproduct of several different soul iniquities, one thing is for sure. People with a critical spirit have lots of pride. That pride makes them think they have a right to judge others. And that pride blinds the person to their own delusional thinking. They believe they are correct in their judgments and criticisms and wouldn't entertain the idea that they could be wrong.

Someone with a critical spirit may accumulate accurate information, but they could still have the wrong conclusions. People with a crucial heart tend to be negative people so their conclusions to situations will usually have a negative spin. What they perceive as fact in a situation may not be the total reality of it because their focus is wrong. For example, when the twelve spies scoped out the land that God had given them, ten of them brought back a negative report (Numbers 13-14). But two of them brought back a positive report. The facts were correct from both the positive and negative spies – that the land was very fertile but there were giants occupying it. The pessimistic, critical spies only saw a negative outcome. Whereas the faith-filled, positive spies focused on how good the land was (flowing with milk and honey) and viewed the giants as a temporary problem.

Being Negative

One of the ways a negative/critical/judgmental mindset can manifest is having a pessimistic outlook. We understand that most people are either negative or positive; they are either pessimistic or optimistic. The general consensus is that people are hard-wired to either be one or the other. It is true that some of the 16 different personality temperament types are more inclined towards one or the other. However, it isn't true that we are destined to be pessimistic or optimistic.

Pessimistic people usually focus on fear and as a result, their mind rehearses all the possible things that can go wrong. However, what we choose to meditate on is absolutely a choice. So being pessimistic is a choice. To stop the cycle of pessimism, we need to make a concerted effort to stop vocalizing all the negative thoughts that assail our minds and choose instead to focus and talk about positive things. The glass doesn't have to be half empty. In fact, when we speak negatively, we curse ourselves and others. We empower dark forces and give permission to the devil to rob, steal, and destroy. Proverbs 18:21 *"Death and life are in the power of the tongue, and those who love it will eat its fruit."* When we speak negatively, we give demons ideas of how to harm us and those we are cursing. They may not have even thought through the negative scenarios that we just blurted out. And unfortunately, as this verse says, we eat the fruit of what we say.

When I was with Coldwell Banker Real Estate in the 90's, there was a man that sat in a cubicle near me. If you were to look at him, you would assume he was very successful. He looked the part. He dressed well, he had a friendly personality, and he seemed trustworthy. However, sitting so close to him, I heard his conversations. He was a new real estate agent, and he lacked experience. Because his confidence level was low, he kept sabotaging opportunities for success. He never asked potential clients for appointments. They were calling the office because they had an interest in a certain property and he never suggested taking them to see the property they called about. He answered questions about the properties but with a negative tone. He assumed the people he spoke with were not ready, willing, or able to purchase a home so he shot potential clients down without even realizing what he was doing. He was so negative on the phone, it made me wonder why he even showed up at the office.

I left Coldwell Banker to start my own real estate brokerage, so I lost touch with him. About a year later, I ran into him. He was working at The Home Depot because he didn't make it in real estate. He ate the fruit of his words. He spoke weakness, lack, and failure and he got what he asked for.

Of course, pessimistic people will self-sabotage themselves. If all you do is speak negativity you will have the fruit of your own lips. You will manifest weakness, lack, and failure into your life.

Summary

What is in our subconscious mind directs our attitudes and actions. *Diseases of the soul* are strongholds, they are like spots of cancer in our soul. They can grow and fester in our hidden, inner man.

If we were to go back to that analogy of our psyche being like a computer, *diseases of the soul* are like computer viruses. They can run in the background without us knowing it, and they can cause major performance issues. As you read in this chapter, they can be the cause of self-sabotage.

Chapter 8

Autopilot Glitches

A glitch is a mistake or irregularity. Do you remember in the first Matrix movie when Neo saw a black cat walk by the doorway, then he saw that exact same thing happen again? He was told that was a *glitch in the matrix* and to beware when that happens. In the movie, when someone experienced a *déjà vu* happening, when something repeated itself, it was a glitch in the Matrix A.I. system.

In the context of this book, a glitch is a repeating thought or behavior. For those of us that are old enough to remember vinyl records, when there was a scratch in the record, it caused the same line to repeat over and over.

Most of us have auto-pilot type behaviors that we repeat even though those thoughts or behaviors are either sinful or self-sabotaging. These glitches (scratches, lines, folds, wrinkles) in our subconscious mind can get triggered when we encounter a situation, emotion, or feeling that we have had in the past. As a result, we just repeat the belief or behavior in almost an auto-pilot manner. These glitches are the fifth root cause of self-sabotage this book will address.

In the last chapter, when describing *diseases of the soul*, I mentioned that they are iniquities that can be autopilot sinful responses where a person often doesn't deliberate a sinful temptation. Most of the time, people sin or self-sabotage without thinking about their behavior. Our glitches do exactly the same thing. Our glitches are autopilot repeating responses embedded into our subconscious mind.

Most of us have some glitch, default, autopilot responses when we encounter certain situations. They could just be our thought process about a situation and not necessarily an action we take. They are programming code errors in our brain that can affect our thoughts or behaviors when we encounter specific situations. They can be a manifestation of a soul iniquity, or they could be a reaction to a situation that we never self-corrected.

For example, a friend of mine had a glitch where she seemed to revert to a three-year-old crybaby child when she didn't get her way with her family. She was normal and emotionally mature the rest of the time, but something happened to her when she was on the phone with her family, and she didn't get her way. She would start crying big crocodile tears and morphed into a child. She didn't cry adult tears. She actually looked like an adult trying to mimic a toddler crying. It was shocking to witness. She didn't just repeat this behavior with her mom and dad, she did it with her older siblings when she wanted something that they wouldn't give her.

I brought this to her attention, and we talked about it. She wasn't aware she was doing it. She knew in her head that she doesn't get her way when she throws a temper tantrum, but her family never called her out on the behavior pattern, so it was her *go to* response. It wasn't something planned, and she wasn't trying to purposely be manipulative. It was simply a childhood behavior that never got corrected.

Another friend of mine would lash out and get mean when she was in certain situations. If she felt that someone or something was coming against or threatening her core necessities, like shelter, she would jump into a *trapped mountain lion* mode. Like a cornered mountain lion, she would lash out and try to hurt anyone that she felt threated by. Sometimes, her reactions were way more aggressive than the situation called for. It was her habit. It was her auto-response when she was triggered in a certain way.

Another guy friend of mine has a glitch programmed

in his subconscious mind that makes him defensive. When he encounters certain triggers, his programming code glitch tells him to react in a hostile and defensive way. If you ask him questions about something to get clarification or if you try to explain something to him, his autopilot response kicks in. He gets triggered and he reacts like he is being attacked. He will even say, "Why are you attacking me?" when I may be giving more details or asking for more details. He realizes he does it, after the fact, but that doesn't stop his initial emotional reaction of feeling attacked.

The "I Need Money" Glitch

A lot of people have a subconscious command that tells them "I need money." The *"I need money"* subconscious blueprint expresses itself as a *poverty mentality* and the person either hoards money or they waste money. The subconscious command or voice in a person's head that tells them that they need money is a neurological imprint that has become part of that person's identity.

Someone that hoards money is extremely frugal regardless of how much money they have. Their fear of being broke causes them to frequently refrain from spending money on themselves or others.

Years ago, one of my mother's caregivers that had also rented a room from us was very frugal. She didn't hoard possessions. In fact, she was a minimalist. Normally, the trait of being careful with money would be a very admirable trait. However, the woman had sold her condo and had over $100,000 in the bank and she still pinched pennies like she didn't have a dime to her name.

She and I and some other ladies went to lunch. When it came time to order, she only ordered the $1.99 scoop of ice cream. I knew she must have been hungry because she hadn't eaten anything earlier. I asked her privately why she only ordered a scoop of ice cream. She said because it costs $1.99, and it was the cheapest thing on the menu. I spent a couple minutes trying to convince her to change her order to the $6.99 lunch special because it was a lot of food for a good price. She had over $100,000 in the bank but she wouldn't reconsider her lunch order.

The *"I need money"* subconscious glitch was well established within my brother Ken, as well. Except with him, it was the opposite from my mother's caregiver. His *"I need money"* subconscious command made him spend, waste, and give away any money. That subconscious command merged into his identity. For him, that wrong blueprint kept replaying the broken record *"I need money"* so he subconsciously sabotaged his circumstances to line up with that command.

There is an old adage, *"You are what you think you are, or you become it."* It's similar to Proverbs 23:7a, which says, *"For as he thinks in his heart, so is he."* If you think you are fat, you will be fat. Even if you weren't heavy when that belief was embraced, over time, it will become your reality. If you think you are poor, you will become poor. Your current existence will align with what you believe about yourself.

Ken had money management issues for as long as I can remember. Even back in the 90's, he would continually ask to borrow money from me. If I were to estimate the total amount he borrowed from me, I would guess that amount to be over $50,000. I say borrow but he never paid any of it back. There were three times when the balance was over $10,000, and I wiped the debt off and started a fresh tally.

He was irresponsible when it came to money management. If he borrowed money for his truck registration, I would have to literally give it to him when he was on his way to DMV. Otherwise, if I gave it to him the day before he went to DMV, he would spend it, waste it, or give it away. He had a habit of rationalizing his money issues. All new expenses would be an emergency and he always told himself he could spend what he had borrowed and the money he would get the following week could cover the cost of whatever he borrowed money for.

He lived with me for seven years in the 2010's when I was the trustee for the family estate after our father passed away. The money he made as an electrician and handyman was mostly given to his female friends in the Philippines. He used to come to me almost daily and ask for $2 to $20 dollars for different items. He didn't pay for food, rent, or utilities in that seven-year period. He was broke all the time. That was his identity. That was his comfort zone even though you would think it would be extremely uncomfortable. It was what he was used to; it was his normal.

When he got big chunks of money, he quickly squandered it. In 2001, he received $10,000 as a portion of our sister Stephanie's life insurance and it was spent within a week. When he received an inheritance amount of $80,000 in 2017, he had spent it in about two and a half months. He bought a cheap truck and a motorcycle. He lived in a Motel 6 for a couple of months, then he sent the rest of it to his friends in the Philippines. He spent about $15,000 to $18,000 on himself and sent the rest overseas.

I have known other people with the same money management challenges that stem from a subconscious *"I need money"* internal command. However, Ken's was so dramatic, it was a good example. When people have this, they usually don't recognize it for what it is. They usually will have reasons and excuses for all their financial decisions. But when an issue isn't recognized then the record player just keeps playing. That scratch on their record causes the same lyrics (behaviors) to just keep repeating.

Pathways in the Brain

Neuroscience tells us that streams of beliefs and patterns of behavior are established pathways in our mind. There are so many pathways that it only makes sense that we have ones that are not beneficial for us. But thank God, neuroscience also tells us we can *train our brain* and replace negative pathways with new positive ones. The biggest problem is most of our negative beliefs or behaviors go unchecked and unchallenged. They are rarely diagnosed. They are usually not understood, so they are not dealt with properly.

A neuroscience instructor who was conducting a training that I attended, called our patterns of behavior *pathways in the brain,* but in my mind, I envisioned them like a complex freeway system. The last time I was in Dallas, I was completely amazed by the complexity of all of the highways, byways, overpasses and offramps in the downtown Dallas area. It was a mess. Even with my navigational app on my phone, I still took wrong exits and ended up on streets I didn't want to be on. I immediately drew a parallel between the Dallas freeway system and the neuroscientist's pathway in the brain. If we think of our patterns of thoughts and behaviors like a giant roadway complex, we can understand how we can keep taking the wrong offramps of negative conclusions and behaviors.

In certain situations, we don't pay attention. Our mind is on other things as we take the roads (pathways) we are familiar with. We have all driven with our minds on other things and we have missed the offramp we had intended to take. We have also driven home on autopilot and forgot that we had intended to run an errand before going home. We weren't thinking about our driving as we were driving. Our mind was on something else. Yet, our internal autopilot kicked in as we thought about something that happened at work. After I moved to my current house, there were a couple of times where I had accidentally driven into my old tract. The same is true for our thought patterns and negative behaviors. We take the offramps we are used to, even if it means we end up at destinations that weren't intended. They are our *normal*. And we are often blind to the fact that we need to establish a new *normal*.

What are our wrinkles/glitches/repeating thoughts and behaviors that are self-sabotaging? Can we identify any of them? With some of them, identifying them is all that is really needed to correct them. With the woman that acted like a child around her family, knowing she did that was enough to cause her to change that behavior. Some wrong patterns can be adjusted by recognizing the triggers and making a choice to respond in a different way. Other default behaviors may be harder to correct but diagnosing them is the first step.

Chapter 9

Stepping Into Success

The title of this chapter is "Stepping into Success" because our success requires steps. We don't just suddenly end up successful. Success is a step-by-step process. We have to take steps and we usually have to complete one step before we are ready for the next step.

Our problem is most of us see the assignment, promise, or goal as a huge mountain. It seems too big in our mind, so we try to put the responsibility on God to perform. We fail to see that we are the one that God assigned the project to and that means we are the one that has to take steps towards it. Our goals usually don't involve just one action. Most of the promises and goals involve several steps before we arrive at the finish line of achievement.

This book covered a lot of information. In this chapter, I want to revisit the content of the different chapters and then offer some keys to breaking the negative cycles.

The Saboteur Within

The first chapter talked about fear, procrastination, weariness, and our flesh nature. These surface level manifestations of self-sabotage are usually not recognized. We don't acknowledge fear as the reason we don't move to a new house, or start school, or ask a woman on a date. We don't label our procrastination as procrastination. Instead, we have other excuses for delaying our steps towards success. When we are tired and weary, we don't even bother with excuses. We don't think about our projects and goals. We are too busy treading water to even consider our goals. And when our indulgent flesh nature rules, we want to let it rule. We don't think about what we should do because we want to enjoy our laziness or gluttony.

Exercise/Assignment:

In a notebook, write out what your goals are. This may take some time to remember them. Try to include the big ones and small ones. Give each goal its own page. Then brainstorm what you think needs to be done for each of the goals. Don't rush it. Maybe only think about one goal per day.

Write down what you want the end result to be and then write all the steps you can think of. Throughout the day, you may think of more steps, so be sure to add those to the journal. You will find that there are a lot of little steps that you can take now. In fact, you may find that 80% of the steps (action items) are little ones that aren't that intimidating.

For example, say the goal is to write a book. Maybe you have been thinking about writing a book for five years, but you still haven't done it. The project feels huge in your mind. What are some steps you can take?

Brainstorm ideas for your book. What is the main topic of the book? What title ideas do you have? Have you researched to see if that title is already taken? Have you researched publishing and self-publishing options? Have you talked to other authors to ask their advice on publishing? Have you researched the number of words your book should be for the genre (type of book)? What are some major points you want to make in the book? Of the points you want to make, which ones should be their own chapter? How is your writing technique? Should you take a class or workshop in writing? What are some ideas for the book cover? Have you asked for guidance from other authors about your book cover ideas? Is there a topic in your book that you should research? Do you know how to research it? Will your book have an introduction? If you are unsure of how to do an introduction, maybe read some introductions from other books to familiarize yourself with them. How many chapters do you want to have? What are the names of your chapters? Are you ready to write some sections now? You don't have to write the sections in order. You can skip ahead and then circle back later. Have you written a brief author biography? Do you have a professional photo of yourself for the back book cover? Have you written the book description that will be printed on the back of the book and will be your meta data for online sales?

As you can see there are lots of little steps that can be taken. Surprisingly, momentum builds as you complete these little steps and your dream of writing a book will soon come to pass if you keep taking the little steps. When you are doing the actual writing give yourself goals. Commit to yourself, "I want to finish chapter one this week, and chapter two next week." Setting goals for yourself will help keep you on track.

If the goal is to start your own business, are there parts of the business you still need to learn before launching it? Do you need any certifications or licenses? Have you read any books or taken any courses on starting a new business? If you are selling products, have you nailed down specifically which type of products you will be selling? Are there additional products to add to your line of inventory? If it's a service business, have you defined exactly what services you provide? What does the competition in your area look like for that type of business? What will set your business apart? How are you going to attract customers? How much will it cost to set up the business? Have you designed your logo? Have you investigated leasing office space, or will you be working from home? Have you researched getting a business license and a Fictitious Business Name from the county you live in? Is it the type of business that you can start small and then build as you grow?

Whatever the goal is, you can't take steps unless you know what the steps are. Your goal will require brainstorming on paper, not just in your head. When you write down an idea, it frees up your mind to move on to the next topic. Keep a running journal of ideas and steps. You won't know all the steps when you start to brainstorm them. As you complete one you often learn about additional steps that are needed. Taking steps towards your goals is an educational journey, and you need to just keep stepping. Because the "to do" list can get long; you can take steps every week towards your goal. Projects become a lot less intimidating as you take small steps towards them.

Understanding Our Soul

The second chapter gave an overview of our psyche. We talked about psychology and the Bible both indicating that our beliefs, behaviors, and motives are driven from our subconscious mind and not our conscious mind.

The Holy Spirit dwells in our human spirit and when the Holy Spirit speaks to us, that message usually travels from our spirit, through our subconscious mind, and is registered as a thought in our conscious mind. We talked about improving our discernment by taking every thought captive, renewing our mind to the word of God, and rooting out the negative thoughts and behavior patterns.

The analogy of a computer was described where our spirit is like a mother board. Our subconscious mind is like a hard drive. Our conscious mind is like a monitor. Our words are like a keyboard which is how we change the programming. Chapter Two talked about how our attitudes, words, and actions reflect what is resident in our subconscious mind.

Exercise/Assignment

Can you think of any examples of something you or someone you know said or did that reflected something they had in their subconscious mind? Did you give money to a homeless person? If you did that would reflect that you have compassion in your heart. Did a co-worker put someone down to make themselves look better? Did they compare themselves to someone? Both of those actions are manifestations of jealousy.

The idea behind this exercise is to begin to pay

attention to behaviors, and to look for motives. We often don't see our true motives. We usually just rehearse our excuses for our actions.

However, having the ability to recognize true motives is something that will benefit you the rest of your life. If you are in management and have that ability, you won't be conned by employees. If you are a parent, you will have more understanding of situations, and will have insights that will help you parent your children.

The Power of Faith

The third chapter taught about faith. Real faith is what we believe in our subconscious mind not mental agreement in our conscious mind. Faith and fear are opposites. Faith is not denial. The chapter talked about our subconscious mind being a *miracle factory* if we are able to get what we believe in our head to sink down into our heart. As well, faith in our subconscious mind can overrule our self-sabotaging tendencies so faith can force our goals into manifestation.

Exercise/Assignment

Remember the experience I shared where I had the abscessed root canal? The Holy Spirit spoke to me and told me it wasn't His will that I be in pain. I meditated and rehearsed that sentence over and over until it sunk down in my heart and I received complete healing within an hour.

What promises has the Holy Spirit spoken to you? Write them down. Then, spend a little time meditating on them. If you can't think of a Rhema promise, then rehearse a logos (written promise from the Bible) in your mind. Remember, our conscious mind is the gateway to our subconscious mind. If we want to plant faith in us or root our negative tendencies, we do it through our conscious mind. Faith comes by hearing and hearing by the word of God. Rehearse and meditate on the word of God for your life.

Deposits of Hope

While we can identify our hopes and aspirations in our conscious mind, our subconscious mind actually carries deposits of hope. Those deposits are the substance that is converted to faith. The analogy was given that hope is like an egg, but faith is a fertilized egg that carries new life.

The definition of hope is a feeling of expectation and desire for a certain thing to happen. Are we expecting the blessing? Are we prepared for it? Do we truly desire it?

Exercise/Assignment

Evaluate your goals and the promises of God in your life. Do you still expect them and desire them?

Have you missed opportunities because you didn't expect them? Are there steps you need to take before you are ready on your end? If so, identify them and take steps towards them.

I mentioned that the topic of hope has been stirring in me for weeks. One thing I haven't mentioned that has been on my mind is the act of *laying on of hands* as it pertains to our deposits of hope in our subconscious mind.

2 Timothy 1:6 says, *"Therefore I remind you to stir up the gift of God which is in you through the laying on of my hand."* 1 Timothy 4:14 says, *"Do not neglect the gift that is in you, which was given to you by prophecy with the laying on of the hands of the eldership."*

The Holy Spirit has been highlighting to me that receiving prayer with the *laying on of hands* from pastors or church elders can rekindle our deposits of hope. It can fan the flames, so our expectancy doesn't die out.

Supernatural transfers and impartations can be done in the spirit realm so let's not treat *laying on of hands* lightly. When we are in a prayer line or we answer an altar call, we are there to do business with God. We are not receiving something from the minister that prays for us. We are receiving a touch from the Holy Spirit who happens to be using a minister to do His bidding.

I am surprised that the Holy Spirit keeps bringing the *laying on of hands* for hope to my mind so often recently. I believe He is encouraging believers to get prayed for so their hopes and dreams get reignited.

Comfort Zones and Boundaries

We have comfort zones and boundaries erected in our subconscious mind that limit our movement in different areas of our life. They can restrict our income, our weight, our friendships, and other areas of our life. They are invisible limitations we unknowingly put on ourselves.

Exercise/Assignment

Reflect on the different areas of your life where you may have subconscious boundaries established. What is the highest and lowest weight your weight has been the last five years? How many times have you been close to your lowest weight? Did you have difficulty dropping under that weight? What has your yearly income been for the last 20 years? What is the highest you made in one year? Could it have been higher in your industry? When it started to get high, did you do things that *took your foot off the gas,* metaphorically?

It may seem strange to you but start doing some affirmations? Put some sticky notes on your bathroom mirror. Write the weight you would like to be and say on the note, "I weigh _____ lbs." Do the same with your income. And every morning read those notes out loud to yourself.

We are trying to change your subconscious comfort zones. Neuroscience tells us we can change the neurological pathways in our brain by the words we say and hear. We can reprogram our comfort zone boundaries, so we stop sabotaging our success.

Ask God to give you a picture of yourself at that new weight, or at that new income. Get that picture in your mind. When you read your sticky notes in the mornings, bring up that memory of what you look like at your goal.

Recognizing Self Blame

The reason I labeled the sixth chapter *Recognizing Self Blame* is that it has been my observation that most people are not aware of when they are carrying unforgiveness towards themselves. It is common for people to carry traumas and dramas, but never emotionally process those events in their lives. They can embrace blame, but never try to understand the situation to see it objectively.

People often misappropriate blame. They either deny all responsibility, or they accept too much of it. It is psychologically healthy to get a factual and accurate assessment of a traumatic event.

Exercise/Assignment

Ask yourself some questions. Was there a major event in your life that was traumatizing? Was it someone's fault? Do you blame yourself for it? Were you a contributing factor?

Human nature wants to brush it all *under the rug,* but in these situations it is important to emotionally process traumatic situations in our life. If we don't, we may be harboring wrong beliefs about it and not recognize it. If a situation was our fault, acknowledge it. Accept the responsibility and move on. Don't dwell on it and allow it to consume all your thoughts. If possible, make amends and apologize. Reflect on things you learned out of the situation. Ask God to forgive you and help heal the situation.

Do not carry unforgiveness towards yourself. Those that do often try to subconsciously punish themselves in self-sabotaging ways.

Diseases of the Soul

In chapter seven soul iniquities were discussed, specially, pride, fear, jealousy, offense, weak willpower, and a critical spirit. *Diseases of the soul* can act like cancers. They can destroy our relationships, business opportunities, and destinies.

Exercise/Assignment

The first step in uprooting a *disease of the soul* is recognizing it. Identify the ways it manifests in our life.

Then, we need to repent of it. Repentance isn't a

quick "forgive me" prayer. Repentance is a breaking of our pride. There is a humbling. Repentance has to be sincere and heart-felt. When we repent it is like we take a sledgehammer and purposely crack the ice of our heart. Just like pride (metaphorically) causes a layer of ice between our conscious mind and our subconscious mind, repentance with humility, cracks that ice. Behaviors are driven from our subconscious mind, so we need to create cracks in our hard hearts in order for us to have true repentance.

As of this writing, there is a popular trend on social media that shows disgusting boils, cysts, and tumors being lanced and squeezed out. It isn't just popping pimples, these videos showcase all kinds of gross eliminations of puss, tumors, and cysts. Repentance is like these videos. If we just say a quick "forgive me" prayer, that is like taking an alcohol swab and quickly brushing over the top of the growth without penetrating the skin. However, if we break the ice of our heart, then it's like we lance the infected sore by cutting through the skin so we can reach the infection.

I know this is a crude analogy, but we need to view our sin as gross and ugly. Soul iniquities are gross soul cancers, and we need to view them that way.

On the videos, we see the boils, pimples, cysts, and tumors being lanced and the bumps or infections are squeezed out. After the cyst is removed, the doctor usually squirts an antibiotic cleansing liquid into the open sore to clean it out. That reminds me of the cleansing of the word of God. When we purge an issue in our heart, we follow it up by treating it with the washing of the Word. Ephesians 5:26 says, *"that He might sanctify and cleanse her with the washing of the word."*

Part of the repentance process is (metaphorically) squeezing and pulling. We are pulling up memories of how we have harmed others by our soul iniquities. We need to observe and understand the consequences of our words and actions and how they have hurt others and sabotaged our own lives. We need to take off the blinders of self-preservation that often causes us not to recognize how much our actions have wounded others and ourselves. We need to face the real truth, not our prideful, self-protective version of the truth.

We have to see the ugly side of an iniquity, other-wise, it is human nature to rationalize that our *pet sins* aren't that bad. We will take the posture that we haven't hurt anyone and no one else even knows about our iniquities. If we don't really believe it is bad, then we won't sincerely repent.

Tether Yourself

The word *tether* means to tie or attach a rope or chain to an animal. For example, a dog can be tethered to a long rope, so it stays in the yard. Of course, we are not animals, but it is good idea to give ourselves a short leash when it comes to our soul diseases. What does that mean? It means any time we recognize a thought or action that could be a manifestation of a *disease of the soul* we have, we need to quickly recognize it and reign it in.

As children, many of us played tetherball which had an eight-foot pole with a six-foot long rope attached to the top of it and a ball was attached to the other end of the rope. Two players would try to hit the ball in opposite directions and the one that was able to get all the rope encircled around the pole would win the point. We would see the ball going in the wrong direction and we would need to swing at it to get the ball going in the right direction. When we keep ourselves on a short leash, we quickly jump into action to hit or correct an action that is going in the wrong direction.

There are some soul iniquities that can be corrected very easily. While there will be others that will be much more difficult. Some Issues, like pride, will be difficult and it will be in stages. We can squeeze out as much as we see, but if that infection is spread out then we aren't going to get it all out our first try.

I understand it seems hard, and the enemy of your soul would try to convince you that it isn't worth the trouble. He would say if a lump keeps growing back, why bother? Well, if you have seen the boils and cysts being popped in these videos, you would see that it is much better to get rid of as much as you can, even if not all of it is extracted at that first office visit. It is better to have a one-inch lump that has grown back than a massive 4-inch mound that was left untreated. The bigger the infection is the more dangerous it is to the body. Likewise, the bigger the soul iniquity is the more damage it can cause to your life.

We need to remember and rehearse Psalm 103:1-4. It reads: *(1) Bless the Lord, O my soul; and all that is within me, bless His holy name! (2) Bless the Lord, O my soul, and forget not all His benefits; (3) Who forgives all your iniquities, who heals all your diseases, who re-deems your life from destruction, who crowns you with lovingkindness and tender mercies."*

God isn't a mean taskmaster. He doesn't demand perfection. He understands the human condition. He comprehends the evils and iniquities that reside in the hearts of men. Just because the contents of this book may be new to you doesn't mean that it is new to God. Humans having pride and sinful motives in their hearts date back to the fall of man. However, God tells us in this verse in Psalms that He forgives all our iniquities, and He heals all our diseases, that means He can even heal our *diseases of the soul.* He sees that we are on a path of destruction, and He delivers us, and even crowns us with lovingkindness and tender mercies.

So even though we may not be instantly zapped perfect after we repent of an area, we shouldn't give up. Remember, our conscious mind is the gateway to our subconscious mind. When we recognize a thought or behavior that isn't right, we stop and correct it, that is how we change the neurological pathways in our brain. That is how we re-write the computer code in our subconscious mind. By keeping ourselves tethered to God's heart, we can easily recognize our carnal behavior patterns. If we are tethered to God's ways, then we will *walk in the spirit.* Galatians 5:16 says, *"I say then: Walk in the spirit, and you will not fulfill the lusts of the flesh."*

So not only does the Bible tell us that wrong behaviors can be corrected, but neuroscience also tells us that as well. They both tell us that old patterns of thoughts and behaviors can be broken, and new patterns can be established. Neuroscience tells us that new neurological pathways can be established in our brain by repeating that new thought or behavior. We can create detours of thoughts and behaviors. At first, that correct thought or behavior may seem like just a hiking path. But after repeated action, it can become a four-lane highway in our brain and become our new normal.

Our character is developed by our choices. When children are allowed to get away with lying, it reinforces the behavior so that particular habit becomes a way of life. The same is true with any character issue. If areas are not confronted then they can become a stronghold in our life and once this occurs, they become second nature. A sin uncorrected will become a habit. A habit unconfronted will become our character.

Autopilot Glitches

In the eighth chapter on Glitches, we talked about our scratch on the record, repeating thoughts or actions which are really just programming errors. In the computer analogy, we said that *diseases of the soul* are like computer viruses on our hard drive. Well, our psychological glitches are like glitches on our hard drive.

Some glitches can get corrected by just recognizing them and what triggers them. It is like when you drive on that complex freeway system, you make a conscious decision that you aren't going to take that offramp. This was the case with my friend that cried like a child when she didn't get her way with her family. She recognized the behavior, and then when the situation rose up again, she refused to throw a temper tantrum and acted maturely.

Other glitches can be more difficult to correct, especially when they have attached themselves to the person's identity. They are harder to correct because the person isn't just erasing a line of coding, they are rewriting an aspect of their identity.

The woman with $100,000 in the bank that wouldn't order lunch had that learned behavior from her family. It was part of her identity. She told me that both of her parents were extremely frugal. For her, it was a *generational curse* that was her normal. It was how she was raised, and she didn't know anything besides hoarding money.

For my brother Ken, wasting money was part of his identity but for different reasons. It fed his ego. If he wasted money on electric guitars or sound equipment (when he couldn't pay his rent) it appeased his ego.

A life goal of his was to create lyrics that would be heard and respected. Giving money to his friends in the Philippines had become his reason for living in the last 15 years of his life. It fed his self-esteem to be the hero of those in need. It made him feel like he was making a difference in the world. They wanted to talk to him. They wanted a relationship with him because he would give them money. Yes, Ken had an "I need money" blueprint that directed his actions, but he also had an underlying factor of feeding his ego.

When evaluating autopilot glitches, whether it be for yourself or a loved one, look for underlying factors that could influence it. With wrong programming that has bonded with a person's identity, understanding those underlying factors can help in correcting the behavior.

Exercise/Assignment

Do you have any autopilot glitches that come out when you get triggered? Is there a situation that makes you jump to conclusions? Do people think you overreach in certain situations?

Examine your behavior. Write down possible repeating thought patterns or behaviors. Do you have any *diseases of the soul* that manifest in a specific way? You can also ask your friends or family if they have noticed any repeating behavior quirks.

Brainstorm aspects of your identity. What do you believe about yourself? Make a list of positive and negative things about your identity. If you have God-given deposits of hope, nurture those seeds. Water them. Do Romans 4:17. *"Call those things that do not exist as though they did."* Reinforce the positive things. Make an effort to ingrain them deeper into your identity. If there are negative beliefs about yourself, write them down. Call them out. Stop letting the enemy reinforce the negative junk. Stop agreeing with the kingdom of darkness about your perceived weaknesses and failures. Speak life to yourself and rehearse positive identity-shaping words to your self-esteem.

Our True Identity

With glitches or any of the other four root causes of self-sabotage discussed in this book, we need to renew our minds to the word of God. We need to embrace the identity that God has for us. Yes, we need to uproot pride and fear, or at least try and minimize those character flaws. However, the most important thing for us to do is to lean into God and develop a more intimate relationship with Him. We need to get God's word in us. The more of His word we hear, the greater our chances that it will sneak down into our subconscious mind. Nothing can stop a person that knows who they are in Christ. Allowing God to change our identity will stop our self-sabotage, so we can be who He has called us to be.